Staff Ride Handbook for Dade's Battle, Florida, 28 December 1835

A Study of Leadership in Irregular Conflict

Captain Michael G. Anderson

Foreword

The Staff Ride Handbook for Dade's Battle, Florida, 28 December 1835 is the eleventh volume in the Combat Studies Institute's Staff Ride Handbook series. Michel G. Anderson's well-researched handbook uses the opening conflict of the Second Seminole War as a vehicle to allow organizations at any echelon to study leadership at the tactical level. Although the battle was part of what is now called "irregular warfare," today's leaders—uniformed and civilian—will find ample opportunity to highlight the role of all warfighting functions with a particular emphasis on intelligence, fires and protection. In addition, the backdrop of two ethno-cultural groups, each antagonistic to the other, provides a strong continuity of experience to the many current and potential future operations of the United States' Armed Forces. Continuing the tradition of CSI Publications and the Staff Ride Handbook series in particular, readers will not be surprised that the insights gleaned from conducting the Dade's Battle staff ride are as relevant today as they were over 175 years ago. Finally, commanders at all levels will find this handbook and the one-day staff ride on which it is based to be an excellent way to enhance subordinates' understanding of their profession. CSI—The Past is Prologue!

Colonel Thomas E. Hanson
Director
Combat Studies Institute

Acknowledgements

No published work is done alone and I wish to thank the many whose efforts and assistance made this possible. The opportunity afforded me by the Combat Studies Institute (CSI) Staff Ride Team for the publication of this study cannot be appreciated enough. First and foremost I wish to thank the outstanding support and assistance provided me by Dr. Curtis S. King of the Staff Ride Team. Without his guidance through the creative and publication process, his insightful suggestions and early readings of the manuscript and invaluable support on the graphics this study would not be the same. Likewise, I wish to thank Dr. Christopher Stowe of the Command and General Staff College (CGSC) Department of Military History for his early reading of the manuscript and suggestions as well. Also, the assistance provided in technical and geographical aspects of the study provided by Mr. George Webb of the Dade's Battlefield Historic State Park and Mr. Patrick Potts of the Hillsborough River State Park and Fort Foster Historic Site was extremely helpful. In addition, I would like to thank the University of Central Florida Army Reserve Officer Training Corps (ROTC) class of 2013 for being such willing and cooperative test subjects for the application of the staff ride handbook. Finally, I wish to thank my close friends and family who continually and without complaint provided encouragement and support throughout the entire process, this could not have been done without it.

Contents

Medical

Intelligence

Introduction

The Drums of War

Orders to March

The March

The Ambush

The Soldiers Rally

Final Assault

The Aftermath

Introduction

Francis Langhorne Dade

George Washington Gardiner

Upton Sinclair Fraser

Ransom Clark

Chief Micanopy

Jumper, or Ote Emathla

Alligator, or Halpatter Tustenuggee

Tables

Introduction

As a vehicle for the education of the military professional, the staff ride has long proven its value. Analysis of a battle or a campaign through an examination of the actual terrain is a concept deeply rooted in military study. In Europe, after the Wars of German Unification, Helmuth von Moltke ingrained staff rides into the training of German general staff officers by posing challenging questions to his cadets during rides of battlefields on which he had achieved his greatest triumphs. In the United States, Captain Arthur L. Wagner made an initial proposal for a staff ride and Major Eben Swift brought the concept to fruition at the General Service and Staff School (the forerunner of the Command and General Staff College [CGSC]) in 1906. The essential elements of Wagner and Swift's staff ride concept included a detailed preliminary study of a campaign followed by an in-depth visit to the sites associated with that campaign. Later pioneers of the staff ride added an integration phase in order to mesh the preliminary and field study phases for further insights into the military profession. Thus, the preliminary, field, and integration phases are the cornerstones of the modern staff ride.

Today, the US Army considers the staff ride an essential aspect of historical education for the modern military professional throughout its system of schools, as well as a crucial facet of the continuing professional development of its officers and noncommissioned officers in line units. The CGSC, the Army War College, and institutions throughout the Army's school system conduct staff rides with the extensive resources necessary to fully execute the preliminary study, field study, and integration methodology. Units outside of the schoolhouse environment can also benefit extensively from staff rides but they often find resources, particularly time, to be more restricted. That is where the staff ride handbook comes in. The handbook is a tool that is particularly useful for the line unit in preparing for a staff ride. It provides background to the campaign, a suggested list of sites to visit (called "stands"), material for discussion at the stands, and advice for logistics support of the staff ride. The intent of this handbook is not to replace the detailed study needed for the ride but it does provide a starting point that should make any organization's preparation easier.

This handbook is one in a series of works from the Combat Studies Institute (CSI) designed to facilitate the conduct of staff rides throughout the Armed Forces of the United States. The foundational document of this series is *The Staff Ride* by Dr. William Glenn Robertson (Washington, DC: Center of Military History Publication 70-21, 1987). *The Staff Ride* describes the staff ride methodology in detail and gives hints that will assist in building any staff ride. Other published handbooks focus on particular battles and campaigns and include works on Chickamauga, Cowpens, Shiloh, and Vicksburg among others. CSI staff ride handbooks can be obtained from the CSI website: http://usacac.army.mil/cac2/csi/csipubs.asp. All of these publications are outstanding tools for the military professional, and anyone for that matter, interested in the detailed study of battles and campaigns. This work on Dade's Battle has borrowed liberally from all of its predecessors, particularly in the organizational outline of the handbook as well as the Introduction and the Integration sections specifically. The author is appreciative of the excellent efforts of previous Staff Ride Handbook authors.

Although there is a considerable connection among all staff ride handbooks, the *Staff Ride Handbook for Dade's Battle, Florida, 28 December 1835*, has some significant differences from other handbooks. First, it is a struggle between a conventional-focused peacetime professional army and a budding irregular force. As such, a staff ride for Dade's Battle is a highly relevant small-unit staff ride at the tactical level and thus is a departure from the more common conventional war staff ride studies. Secondly, this battle was a tactical defeat for the US forces as well as the opening battle in a long war with severely limited firsthand accounts. These factors create unique challenges and opportunities.

One of the aspects that sets Dade's Battle apart from other staff rides is the small level of the action which was essentially a couple of hundred combatants on both sides. By necessity, this limits much of the operational analysis typical of many staff rides. Though there exists significant operational-level topics to be discussed in the events leading to the small unit action, it is essentially a study of company-level and lower leadership and tactics between a conventional force and an unconventional foe with the inherent lessons and observations of warfare in an insurgency. This case is the opening battle of such a conflict.

Another challenge is the paucity of firsthand accounts, limited to only one account from a US Army survivor, one from a Seminole chief, and one from a noncombatant translator. This demands that research include a broad analysis of a range of firsthand accounts of later actions in the Second Seminole War as well as reliance on reports from the Soldiers who first arrived on the scene of the battle's aftermath to reconstruct the details of the engagement. Along with the few firsthand accounts, an analysis of the Soldiers' reports on seeing the battlefield and later accounts of the fighting of the war itself, certain secondary sources are integral as well. In addition, as with all insurgency-involved studies, a study of anthropological sources concerning the insurgents is necessary to better understand their approach to the conflict, resources, and organization. This is a point to be emphasized throughout the study but certainly during the preliminary study and integration. Also, to study a defeat instead of focusing only on successes provides an important vehicle for both immediate edification but also a lesson in the art of learning. Of course, the needs and intentions of the staff ride leader will definitively shape the end result of this and any staff ride.

This handbook is structured for a single day's ride with less than 10 stands. Staff ride leaders may have to modify the stands to fit their schedules, and routes, but they should always attempt to keep a sense of connection between stands so that students do not lose the larger context of Major Dade's march. However, due to time constraints, units may choose to execute a battlefield site only study. This handbook is designed to allow staff ride leaders to pick selected stands that perhaps focus on either the entire march or just the battlefield itself as time permits.

In addition, staff ride leaders must give the students a chance to conduct research and prepare before actually visiting the campaign locations. The extent of student preparation will depend on available time. At one end of the spectrum, students might have ample time to explore the secondary sources and even access certain available primary sources such as the passages regarding the battle in John Sprague's *Origin, Progress and Conclusion of the Florida War* (Broadway, N.Y.: D. Appleton and Company, 1837) or John Bemrose's *Reminiscences of the Second Seminole War* (Edited with an Introduction and Postscript by John K. Mahon, University of Tampa, FL, Tampa Press, 2001). On the other hand, if students have less time to devote to research, Frank Laumer's *Dade's Last Command* (Gainesville, FL, University Press of Florida, 1995) provides an excellent account of the entire march and background. The *Staff Ride Handbook for Dade's Battle* provides a systematic approach to the analysis of this long overlooked battle.

Part I describes the organization of the United States Army of the Frontier and what little is known of the Seminole Nation, detailing their weapons, tactics, logistics, engineer, communications, medical support, and intelligence gathering.

Part II consists of a campaign overview which establishes the context for the individual actions to be studied in the field.

Part III consists of a suggested itinerary of sites to visit in order to obtain a concrete view of the campaign in its critical moments. For each stand, there is a set of travel directions, an orientation to the battle site, a discussion of the action that occurred there, vignettes by participants in the campaign, and suggested analysis questions and topics for discussion.

Part IV discusses the final phase of the staff ride, the integration phase. In this phase, students integrate the classroom portion of the staff ride with the field phase and seek to provide relevant lessons for the modern military professional.

Part V provides practical information on conducting a staff ride in the Tampa and Dade Battlefield area, including sources of assistance and logistical considerations.

Appendix A outlines the order of battle for the forces involved on the day of battle. Appendix B provides biographical sketches of key participants, and appendix C provides historical maps of the area. A bibliography suggests sources for preliminary study.

In sum, the Dade's Battle campaign is a magnificent example of small unit leadership and tactics between a conventional force and its unconventional foe and the price paid by the common soldier. The lessons that may be learned from this small but complex struggle can provide a superb tool for the education of the modern military professional.

Part I. Second Seminole War Opponents

United States Army Organization

Peacetime Army

Overview

The aversion of the United States to a standing army meant that there was only a limited cadre of professional Soldiers and officers during "peacetime." This aversion stemmed in large part from a tradition rooted in English history--the puritanical reign of Oliver Cromwell's New Model Army in England. The use of this professional standing army for the enforcement of a specific sect of society's views on the rest of the country resulted in a deep-seated fear in English political thought of a permanent fulltime land force at the control of a few individuals. In the political tradition of their former colonial masters, the United States inherited this aversion. The new nation thus relied on a surge of volunteers or militia forces to fill out the ranks for any major conflict. This type of force would take time to enroll, organize, and train, leaving the meager professional army to bear the brunt of the conflict's opening battles.

As of 9 December 1835, the US Army was composed of 6,595 enlisted Soldiers led by 603 commissioned officers. The regimental breakdown was one regiment of dragoons, four regiments of artillery, and seven regiments of foot infantry with non-regimental affiliated engineers and staff accounting for the rest of the Army (see Table 1). This army was scattered over 53 separate posts with no single gathering of more than 10 companies in one place.

Table One:
United States Army
(as of 9 December 1835)

Regimental Affiliation	Number of Regiments	Number of Soldiers
Dragoons	1	749
Artillery	4	2,180
Infantry	7	3,829
Non-affiliated	N/A	440
Total	12	7,198

The focus of the peacetime military was dominated by the diplomatic gamesmanship between President Andrew Jackson and France which ultimately placed an emphasis on the United States Navy and coastline fortifications of the United States. The quarrel was over a promise from France to pay recompense to the United States for damages done to United States ships during Napoleon Bonaparte's rule of France. When France neglected to fulfill this pledge, President Jackson proceeded to seek Congressional approval to punish France for their lack of payment. In turn, France was offended by such an illicit threat to its interests bringing the two nations precipitously close to open naval warfare and thus putting military focus in the United States to the Navy and to the defense of the shores. This resulted in less of a focus on the defense of the territories and frontier, and more of a containment approach to the trouble with the "Indian Question".

The US Army presence in Florida was significant in light of the relative size of the Army. There were 536 Soldiers serving in Florida, of which 26 were commissioned officers. These were scattered over less than ten posts and mostly congregated in north-central Florida with the exception of the post at Key West. Leading up to Dade's Battle there was growing concern over increasing violence. However, the US Government dismissed many of the fears and warnings from those in the Florida Territory itself and was slow to respond. Although nowhere else in the United States were more than ten companies co-located, the Secretary of War in 1835, Lewis Cass, ordered reinforcements of Regulars to be sent to Florida to bring Florida's total up to 14 companies of Regulars. This reinforcement would not be completed before the outbreak of hostilities but it did manage to get the necessary movements started. By the end of the war, every US Army Regular regiment had rotated through and seen combat in the war in Florida even as the professional army saw extensive expansion as a result of the war. In addition, the Secretary of War authorized federal appropriations for raising local Florida Volunteer Militia in December. The initial call was for a month's duty for 150 mounted Floridians to bolster the Army in Florida's lack of mounted mobile forces and local knowledge of the area.

Volunteers from across the United States as well as increased numbers of Florida militia volunteers would play a significant role alongside that of the Regulars in the coming Second Seminole War. However, there would be none present at Dade's Battle, who all would be Regulars stationed in Florida.

The Soldiers stationed in Florida, a prism of the entire Regular Army of the day, were mainly foreigners among the enlisted along with hard luck citizens and adventure-seekers. In this period, a skilled laborer was said to have been able to make a dollar a day for his labor whereas the average enlisted Soldiers received only five dollars a month for their duty, although for better or worse, the Soldiers were provided uniforms, food, and housing.

Leadership

The majority of leaders in this small professional army prior to the war came from the United States Military Academy at West Point, New York. The younger junior leaders came from the Academy while many of the older career officers came from other sources. Some officers had obtained battlefield commissions during the War of 1812 and risen from the ranks of the enlisted on merit or connection but few of these made a career of the Army and in peacetime moved to other professions, as did some West Point graduates. Of the 14 general officers in 1835, none were Academy graduates, though this may be due to the youthfulness of the Academy at the time, having only been teaching for 32 years.

The officer class was educated and from upstanding families although even they were paid poorly compared to their civilian peers with similar educations and upbringing. Especially true of the Academy graduates, most officers were not driven by wealth to the colors but rather by ideals and virtues associated with military service as an officer. One other wrote that it was to be "among the elite few, the brave, and honorable spirits" that he joined (John K. Mahon, 118-119). For many, including the author of the above words, this soon gave way to a bitter reality of a nation's indifference and little respect for a professional military class and, of course, the very real effect of a small salary.

The education received at West Point was focused mainly on officership, engineering, and the tactics of a conventional, linear, European-style conflict. Many of the officers had prior experience in both the large-scale War of 1812 against the British and native allies as well as numerous "Indian" wars along the frontiers of the expanding nation. As a result, even though they were a small cadre, the leadership of the period possessed direct experience in many cases in both large-scale conventional warfare as well as "Indian" fighting along the frontier. However, even with this experience, the cultural influences of the period deeply affected the perceptions on and the opinion of these unconventional conflicts with the various tribes. These cultural influences strongly affected the devotion to and retention of lessons and knowledge concerning unconventional warfare.

Major Dade's Soldiers

As they marched on, Dade's command was composed of 100 enlisted men, mostly "red-legged infantry" (an acknowledgement of artillery-trained Soldiers performing infantry duties due to the lack of enough trained infantry to garrison the frontier), and seven combat arms officers with one medical officer attached. Virtually all the enlisted had direct ties to foreign soil, earning their way in America through military service, though some were multi-generation lower class native-born Americans. The young officers were from West Point while the two senior officers, Major Francis Langhorne Dade and Captain Upton Sinclair Fraser, were not. They had one wagon which carried the majority of their food stores and ammunition since artillerymen had no cartridge boxes but rather used improvised cartridge sacks tied to their webbing. In addition, they had the translator and one critical six-pound cannon and caisson. With this force, they entered the Seminole Nation during a growing escalation of hostility.

The US Army Regulars wore sky blue uniforms with white cross-belts forming an X across their chest and back. They wore black leather caps and in winter time, a blue wool-like overcoat. In summer, they wore a white linen shirt. Occasionally, the Soldiers would darken the white cross-belts with charcoal or something similar but it is doubtful that that precaution would have been taken at the time as official hostilities had not been declared. Each carried with him his knapsack, rolled blanket, musket and cartridge box, and limited supply of rations, the excess for the ten-day excursion kept in the wagon.

Weapons

Firearms

The US Soldier carried the standard shoulder-carried weapon of his day, a non-rifled muzzle-loading musket. It was the 1816 model .69 caliber weapon with an effective range between 100 and 200 yards, firing a rounded 120 grain powder musket ball. This model was roughly 58 inches long (without bayonet) and weighed eight to 10 pounds (depending on size/weight of bayonet). The socket bayonets varied of the period for the Model 1816 between 16-21 inches in length, to include the three inch socket.

The drill loading procedure was a six step process.

1. The hammer would be half-cocked.

2. The pan was primed by pouring powder into the pan and closing the frizzen.

3. The remaining powder was poured down the muzzle.

4. The musket ball and the paper wadding were then inserted.

5. The ramrod was used to pack down the ball and wading down the muzzle.

6. The rammer would be removed and the weapon ready to be fired.

(George Webb, "Dade Battlefield Staff Ride Questions." Message to Michael Anderson. 19 December 2012. E-mail).

The standard rate of fire for a skilled experienced soldier was one round every 20 seconds or three times a minute. The officers carried similar flintlock pistols. The common pistol model was an 1819 .54 caliber pistol with 40 grain powder ammunition. It weighed three pounds and was 14 inches long. Effective range for the pistol was roughly 20 yards. Both loading procedure and standard rate of fire for the officers' pistols was the same as that of the shoulder arm.

It must be considered that though there were more modern arms available for the time, just not with Dade's command, they were not seen as the technological solution. The standard alternative to the musket was the model 1819 Hall's breach loading rifle. However, Soldiers who used these in the field complained of the recoil breaking the stocks, of a faulty breechblock that seized up after only a few shots, and that the smaller caliber it fired was not damaging enough to bring a target down effectively. Some of these problems may in fact have been due to a lack of proper training as the breech-loading rifle naturally involved more technical training for proper use as it was a more intricate machine than the traditional muzzle-loader. Even with these complaints from the soldier, the rifle did have a reported four times faster rate of fire, if it did not seize up of course. In addition, it had four times further range and the smaller caliber allowed for more rounds to be carried due to the lighter weight and smaller size. This would allow the Soldiers with a Hall's model rifle to fire four times as many rounds at target four times more distant and having more ammunition, thus allowing for a more prolonged intensity of fire. However, the propensity for prolonged intense fire with more rapid firing weapons would place a significant strain on an inherently weak logistical system. The demand for increased ammunition to supply rapid-firing individual Soldiers would be difficult for the industrial base of the early 1830s to support. Even the rifles available to Dade's men were not well received by the soldiery. At the time of Dade's march, the US Army had roughly one of these breach loading rifles for every 20 muskets, however, there are no records indicating that any rifles were with Dade's command.

Edged Weapons

The officers were armed with straight artillery officer swords or the slightly curved infantry officer sword while the assigned cannon crew carried short swords. None carried the curved sabers of the mounted dragoon. The enlisted men were normally armed with bayonets, certainly if they were infantry, as this was a sign of distinction. However, the non-infantry enlisted, such as the "red-legged" infantry, were not always armed with this critical melee weapon. It was not standard practice to issue anyone, other than infantry, the fearsome bayonet for attachment to the muzzle of their muskets for close combat. Though there were a few true-blue infantrymen in Dade's column, it is reasonable to assert that bayonets were present even among the red-legged infantry. However, the issue of the bayonet as a portion of the Soldiers' weaponry is largely muted as the Seminole were known to avoid close combat, perhaps out of a sense of tactics but for many of the contemporary Soldiers it was sometimes attributed to their diminutive upper-body stature as compared to the physically larger US Soldiers. They were noted to be poor wrestlers in competitions at local forts against US Soldiers and throughout the later Second Seminole War, close combat with hatchets, tomahawks, and the like were extremely rare. An organized and coordinated bayonet charge would disperse gathered Seminoles without a contest as it did each time executed later in the war but the nature of the unconventional war made this occurrence rare.

Artillery

A true projectile weapon that separated the US Army Soldiers from the Seminole Warriors was the presence of the single six-pound cannon. The cannon, though solitary in this case, cannot be underappreciated as both a deadly physical weapon as well as a psychological weapon. It both demoralized the enemy and encouraged friendly forces. Though the majority of Soldiers marching with Dade were "part-time" infantry, they were trained and professional artillerymen, thus they knew how to handle the cannon properly. Even if the deadly impact could be minimized by lack of maneuverability and its solitary state, the cannon's psychological aspects were substantial as the red-legs counted on. However, ammunition was finite for both the cannon and the muskets.

The standard six-pound cannon of the period was animal drawn and weighed approximately 750 pounds. Its range was determined by a combination of powder charge, ammunition type, and elevation. Due to the haste of reacting to an ambush without proper time to place the gun in standard operations, the artillerymen accompanying Major Dade would have fired a quicker loading 1 1/4 pound powder charge at zero elevation resulting in an average range of 318 yards. In ideal conditions, however, with more powder charges and differing elevation and terrain, light pieces such as the six-pounder could reach approximately 1,000 yards.

The standard loading procedure for a six-pounder in action was a nine-step process. The cannon team would be divided into 10 roles with one non-commissioned officer, two gunners, and six junior enlisted loaders.

1. The first command was "Parade!" to which the cannon team took takes their places. Two loaders on each side accompanied by one gunner with two other enlisted men forming a chain from the ammunition carriage to the gun with the non-commissioned officer and an officer standing behind the gun giving commands and assisting with aiming the weapon. At this time, if the gun was not already unhooked from the limbers, the command "Unlimber!" would be given and the team would unhook the cannon and maneuver it into its firing position.

2. The second command was "To Action!" The crew at this time stepped forward preparing to execute the first action upon the cannon.

3. The third command "Sponge Tend, Vent!" was issued and the cannon bore was sponged while the charge was passed from the crate to the gun. Meanwhile, a gunner stepped forward and reached to the breech of the gun and covered the vent.

4. The fourth command was "Handle, Cartridge!" The prepared cartridge was passed from the ammunition bearer to the loader near the cannon.

5. The fifth command was "Charge, Piece!" The cartridge was placed into the bore and the loader with the rammer readies his piece.

6. The sixth command was "Ram down, Cartridge!" which was when the cartridge was rammed down one to two times.

7. The seventh command was "Prime!" at which time the gunner removed his hand from the covering vent and inserted tube until it entered

the cartridge. If not using tubing, the gunner could also insert priming wire to achieve same results as using the tube.

8. The eighth command was "Take, Aim!" The gunner removed his hand from tubing or priming wire and using his fingers ranged the weapon and adjusted as needed the elevation and traverse of piece.

9. The final command was "Fire!" at which time the crew cleared the wheels to avoid recoil and the cannon was lit. Upon firing, the gunner tended to the vent while the rest of the crew awaited instructions as to follow on duties.

(Amos Stoddard, *Exercise for Garrison and Field Ordnance Together with Maneuvers.* New York: Pelsue & Gold, 1812. Section V).

The standard rate of fire for a well-trained crew was up to three rounds per minute or one every 20 seconds. However, for crew safety and to keep the gun from overheating, the normal rate was two rounds per minute or one every 30 seconds. When taking into account the effects of conducting these actions under intense direct fire as with the ambush of Dade's men, it is more likely to err on the side of one round a minute.

Ammunition for the six-pounder was composed of three types. These were canister, solid (or round shot), and grape. Both canister and grape were used for close quarters such as clustered infantry or mounted forces threatening the immediate friendly lines. Grape could be fired as far as 500 yards but canister and grape were more commonly used at closer than 250 yards. The only difference between these two types was what composed the rounds themselves. Canister was a random assortment of shrapnel placed into a container while grape was a collection of rounded musket ball-like projectiles. The third type of round was the solid shot. This was used primarily against fortifications or dense formations of troops at longer range or counterbattery fire. This type of round was more commonly used at ranges exceeding 600 yards. The precise breakdown of the ammunition accompanying Dade's six-pounder is not known, however, it is recorded that they carried a total of 50 rounds for the cannon. In comparison, the standard load for this weapon during its use in the War of 1812 was 90 solid shots and 30 canisters. The peace and logistics of the frontier had certainly curbed artillery ammunition supply for the US Army.

Tactics

Tactical Doctrine of 1835

The US Army's standard drill for tactics was largely based on General Winfield Scott's oversight of the 1824 tactical board along with Commandant of the Cadets William Worth's light infantry drill implemented in West Point instruction. The 1824 tactical board was dominated by traditional, European linear, close-order warfare, the so called "line infantry" in contrast to the more independent "light infantry". The light infantry drills that were included in the revised infantry tactics were largely based on Commandant Worth's instruction at West Point and field tested by both cadets and Soldiers from the artillery school at Fort Monroe. Even with this deviation from a European focus on close-ordered line infantry in contrast to the rare European light infantry, these US Army light infantry (skirmisher) drills were founded in traditional linear tactics and more of an addendum than a standalone concept. Just as in Europe, General Scott could not move himself to specialize a light infantry corps but rather proposed more extensive training of line infantry to have the secondary capabilities of light infantry but always remaining firmly rooted in their traditional duties as close-ordered line infantry. There would be more changes incorporated in the 1835 revision of the US Army Infantry regulations. These were not revolutionary changes but changes nevertheless providing more freedom of maneuver and range for the light infantry and codifying the open order lessons learned in the intermittent frontier conflicts of expanding US influence in North America. The concept of linear formation fighting was still the predominant tactic taught at the US Army's Academy at West Point and from the experiences of the War of 1812, although the addition of an American battlefield influence of light infantry was acknowledged and trained as an addendum to the conventional line infantry instruction. The 1824 and subsequent 1835 revision of the US Army infantry regulations would spark multiple professional debates in the early and mid-1800s, much of it predicated on the constant struggle between frontier fighting advocating a move towards more light infantry drill and the traditional approach to following European models, vacillating between British and French options. The end result would be a hybrid of European style line infantry drill influenced by American light infantry drill based on frontier conflict.

Frontier Tactics

At times necessity dictates tactics rather than institutional doctrine. No one knows more than the soldier on the ground, living in the immediate presence of the "fight" to know just how he needs to train in order to survive. After all, it is his natural survival instincts that are involved. The Florida territory US Army Regulars appeared to be an example of this. These Soldiers according to Private John Bemrose, stationed at Fort King, practiced "drilling in the woods at Indian fighting" as well as marksmanship training. (Bemrose, 25). There is no record of how often or how prolific this sort of training was but it does illuminate the fact that the Soldiers and officers on the frontier knew the necessity of being able to fight in the current terrain, not the terrain of the open Europe-based manuals. Though the institutional denigration of fighting unconventional wars was prominent, many recognized the importance of modified tactics to fit the frontier. Frontier tactics were dominated by the most common soldier at the time along the frontier, the foot soldier. "Frontier tactics" for the infantryman were essentially light infantry, or skirmisher, tactics. This meant more individuality in the soldier's selection of cover, his rate of fire, and target selection. This was still conducted within the confines of officer and Non-Commissioned Officer command and control but in the looser model found in the period's light infantry doctrine. When using these frontier tactics, Soldiers would no longer adhere to a tight linear formation but split into smaller groups and individuals to best use terrain.

These frontier tactics, the woodland drills, would largely supplant the traditional linear tactics with rapidity in the Second Seminole War and indeed, the Soldiers under Major Dade would demonstrate the woodland drill for the majority of the battle before construction of the breastworks.

Logistical Support

Logistics for the US Army of Florida Territory in the mid-1830s was haphazard. Most of the supplies that were not self-cultivated by the scattered posts and settlers were transported into the main posts that served as ports such as Fort Brooke at Tampa Bay, Key West in the south, and St. Augustine on the east coast. For ground logistical support for the more rural and interior posts such as Fort King, rudimentary roads were connected to crisscross the frontier both allowing for transport of goods as well as communication and military maneuver. On these roads the primary logistical mover was the ox or horse-drawn wagon. These supply columns transporting goods between military posts were always vulnerable, in times of war or peace, to marauding bands of Seminoles or criminal settlers. The artillery units were known for using wagons to transport their goods. Even though they were pressed into a more infantry-type role on the frontier, they still were logistically equipped for their more traditional role and thus were supported by more wagons. In contrast, the infantry, and later the dragoons when they were were deployed to Florida, were supported more by pack mules when operating apart from a column that included artillery.

The treaty stipulations that granted the Seminoles the interior of the peninsula as their Seminole Nation and gave the United States the coastlines and limited interior penetration, greatly hampered the logistical situation of the scattered military posts as did the extreme nature of the swampy interior of the peninsula itself. As operations progressed in the Second Seminole War, logistics would increasingly be borne by the growing riverine US Navy boats as they navigated swampy channels, rivers, and streams in support of the US Army. Food, medicine, and ammunition would always be an issue as logistical failures and inabilities crippled even the most experienced Army general's campaign plans in the hitherto unknown terrain and climate of interior Florida.

As for Major Dade's command, once they departed Fort Brooke, they lacked even moderate logistical support. The route of march along Fort King Road took the column deeper into the interior of both the territory and into the Seminole Nation denying them logistical resupply. They took a wagon with them to carry additional ammunition and food for a cumulative 10 days supply. For this march, Dade's command took 30 rounds per person for their personal weapons and 50 rounds for the cannon. This was half of what Dade had taken on a previous march through Seminole territory years earlier as a captain. At that time he took no cannon to account for speed and each of his infantrymen carried 60 rounds of ammunition per person. They made this previous march without contest along the same route from Fort Brooke to Fort King. For sustenance, Dade's command in 1835 took on their person 18 ounces of stale bread, and 3/4 of a pound of raw pork or 1/4 pound of salted or fresh beef. The additional rations for the march were stored on the supply wagon. There was no concerted plan for resupply during the march. The command took a 10-day supply which was to suffice to get them to Fort King where they would resupply and continue operations. For all intents this meant that the only thought for beyond the 10-day supply would be to live off the land as there would be no friendly settlements within the Seminole Territory with which to trade. A 10 day supply of sustenance was a regular occurrence during this period on the frontier in Florida. Generally, half would be carried by the Soldiers on their backs and half the ration in a supply wagon. When resupply was coordinated for during that march, it was generally acquired from locals or mostly from waterborne resupply from a riverine force. This lack of extensive logistical network in support of the march resulted in a critical dearth of ammunition in light of the intensive contact.

Engineer Support

A primary purpose for the creation and sustainment of the military academy at West Point was to provide the nation with a corps of competent and trained engineers. These engineers were largely utilized in peacetime after the War of 1812 to build, restore, and improve on coastal fortifications and did not see much utilization or action in the frontier wars which in comparison to the coastal fortification mission, were a lesser priority. The major contribution of the engineers to the frontier in Florida was the construction of the few roads that did in fact exist such as the critical Fort King Road, although, even these roads were generally constructed by the posted infantry and artillery units.

In Dade's command there were no engineer troops and he had no engineer support other than the academic training of the young West Point graduates. When the command was forced to ford rivers after Seminoles burned the log bridges and move their cannon and wagon through the terrain it was up to the infantrymen, artillerymen, and the officers to conceptualize and execute the mobility and counter-mobility issues.

Communications

Communication within the US Army was either from a verbal messenger or from an official courier delivering written communications. These could be either land-based, being either foot movement or mounted, or seaborne with the messenger or courier transported by ship. The majority of settlements at this time on the Florida frontier dotted the coastline as the previous treaties had provided the Seminoles with the interior portions of the peninsula as their "Seminole Nation" thus the majority of communication along the frontier was passed with merchant ships although land based road networks were beginning to be used but this involved more danger from marauding Seminoles or criminal settlers.

The Fort King Road on which Major Dade's command marched was a major landline of communication from Fort Brooke on the west coast at Tampa Bay with the more eastern Fort King. This road cut through the heart of the Seminole Nation though it was the most direct route between the two forts and divided US Army Regulars in north-central Florida. At the time Major Dade's contingent departed Fort Brooke for Fort King, the land-bound communication between the two forts had been cut off by growing Seminole depredations which included the murder of a US Army courier along the Fort King Road. Throughout the march, Major Dade would receive and send courier-born messages back to Fort Brooke but nothing would come from Fort King.

Within the command, the leaders relied on personal verbal commands. In the period, drums and bugles were utilized regularly in infantry organizations, however, Major Dade's command, perhaps due to its smaller size, neglected this and relied on verbal communication.

Decisions had to be made by officers in the Second Seminole War based on the latest message delivered by ship or courier and both were unreliable in timeliness.

Medical

The military frontier post normally had a serving surgeon from the Army Medical Department assigned to it. Although medical capabilities were limited in the 19th Century and even more so at austere frontier posts, minimal medical knowledge and care was available. The largest medical issue dealt with in peacetime and war was illnesses to include dysentery, measles, mumps, smallpox, rampant malaria, and simple malnutrition. The doctors and their assigned supporting medical orderlies spent much of their time combating pestilence and the rest of it servicing battlefield wounds and local needs. The medical services were not strictly military either. Though the medical personnel were commissioned officers and the orderlies were enlisted Soldiers from the ranks assigned to support the medical professionals, they served the local population as well. There was no progressive medical care in the territories beyond the local post's infirmary. If it could not be handled at the infirmary level of the fort, there were limited options revolving around available transport on merchant vessels to more developed medical facilities.

The US Army Soldiers under Major Dade had Assistant Surgeon Dr. John S. Gatlin accompanying them. Dr. Gatlin was the assigned medical professional to Fort Brooke, and he accompanied the march with a limited supply of bandages and medicine along with his saws and knives contained in his medical bag. He had only just arrived at Fort Brooke from Fort Pickens, near Pensacola, Florida, and after handing off the supplies he had brought with him, he was ordered to accompany Major Dade's column to deliver receipts and invoices to Fort King for medical supplies for Assistant Surgeon Dr. Henry Lee Heiskell. With the extreme lack of supplies and assistance, Dr. Gatlin could only provide rudimentary aid to the wounded in Dade's Battle and, by nature of the fight, be a combatant as well.

Intelligence

US Army intelligence was markedly absent concerning the Seminoles and was not organized or considered in any manner. Through regular postings to the frontier and the First Seminole War, many of the officers and enlisted Soldiers had experience with the Seminoles. As with any garrison or occupational duties, these previous experiences for better and for worse affected judgments and would result in preconceived notions. At the time of the march, most of the information the US Army possessed came from reports from terrified settlers coming to the forts. These settlers were "terrified" from the depredations of the Seminole to include theft, burnings, and posturing of violence. In addition, the garrison forces could witness from their encampments acts of bravado by bands of Seminole in defiance of the agreements. Finally, the US Soldiers also relied heavily on warnings and reports of Seminoles themselves both from boastful antagonists as well as friendly informants. As for physical intelligence gathering, there was a distinct lack of reconnaissance patrolling prior to the hostilities.

Major Dade utilized an African-American slave named Louis Pacheo. Pacheo accompanied him on his march to run ahead as a scout each day for the Seminoles but Pacheo, with later questioned loyalties, never saw any Seminoles though reported there were certain signs such as burned bridges and slaughtered animals. Major Dade's command had also been given the son of a loyal Seminole chief to accompany them but through fear, he had left days before the ambush of the column. The US Army attempted to use the supportive locals as much as possible. Later the regular Army would rely heavily on the untrained Florida Militia for terrain knowledge. Language barriers would consistently be an issue with intelligence gathering as virtually no Army Soldiers spoke the Seminole language and thus they had to rely on either slaves, such as Pacheo, or "loyal" Seminoles to serve as translators.

The Seminole Nation Organization

Pre-war

Overview

Estimates place the Seminole population in 1835 to be approximately 4,000-5,000 with around 500-1,400 warriors among them (Mahon, 121-122). Though commonly referred to as the "Seminole Nation", the organization was more of a confederacy of many different, scattered, and independent tribes that themselves had broken off from the Lower Creek tribes of the Muskogee in Georgia and Alabama. The confederation was nominally ruled by a senior male chief of the oldest and most "original" Seminole tribe of northern Florida. Though there was a council of chiefs and a head chief, the Seminole Nation still was a loosely-based nation of tribes. These tribes did come together in times of need for a greater good but in no manner were they organized in a Western sense of socio-cultural organization. They were said to be proud of their valor and hardiness and to be haughty to outsiders but generally receptive and hospitable.

These Seminoles were offset by the presence of both free Africans, known as "Maroons" who were incorporated and lived peacefully in the Seminole territory, as well as African slaves. The Maroons were separate but included in the loose confederation that made up the Seminole community. They numbered only a few thousand at the time of the Second Seminole War but were well known for their bravery, courage, and violence. In addition, they provided the Seminoles with translators and a deeper understanding of the "white man." The Seminoles were thought to have nearly 100 slaves among them. They embraced a perception of the importance and prestige that slavery provided, having learned this in lower Georgia before the Seminole migration to Florida. These slaves were generally results of military conquests although with more interaction with the Spanish, English, and then Americans, it began to reflect more of an economic idea as well.

By the nature of their society, the Seminoles did not have anything reflective of a standing or professional army. The tradition of the Seminoles when going to war was one of long deliberation and voluntary tribal commitments to the overall war effort. The main hereditary chiefs of the major clans or sub-tribes would come together and once deciding on war, would send envoys out to the smaller tribes with requests for support in supplies and manpower and would declare when the hostilities would commence. This would be done by depositing red sticks at the meeting lodges of each tribe with one stick representing a day. Each day, one stick would be removed in a countdown allowing the tribes to gather the volunteers and donations and deliver them to the hereditary chiefs before the day the war was to begin. Any excesses were stored or returned when the warriors left for war. The lack of a professional system and strong central disciplinary measures meant that Seminole campaigns were never intended to be ones of length and endurance.

Leadership

Seminole leadership was both hereditary and merit-based. The tribal decision-making and the policy-makers were mainly hereditary based. The merit-based leaders were mostly the men of action in the tribes and they led through their influence on the hereditary leadership. The merit-based leaders were the more physical leaders and thus more prominent in military matters. However, even in this, the cultural significance and influence of the hereditary tribal leaders could not be discounted as their presence was integral to any tribal actions, military or not. Although the Seminoles certainly had no professional military education or promotion system they still contained natural and experienced leaders along with the less capable.

The Second Seminole War was not the first armed conflict between the United States and the Seminole Nation in Florida. The First Seminole War had been fought from 1816-1819. Many Seminoles, if they did not have direct experience from the previous conflicts or occasional depredations with the settlers, certainly had heard stories and lessons of previous fights with the Soldiers from their seniors. This allowed for Seminole leadership to have limited knowledge of previous fighting experience but they certainly all knew the land they lived on and what they were fighting to maintain.

The Seminole war chiefs lacked much authority over the tribe-provided warriors other than example and use of shame or glory to inspire. The harsh and stark goals the US Government was enforcing through violence did slightly alter the "traditional" approach to war. In this case the result of failure did inspire some more attempts at enforcing discipline by Seminole war chiefs, exemplified by the Seminole war chief Osceola's threats to kill any warrior who left the fight without his permission. This was the exception and not the rule to Seminole military measures.

Micanopy's Warriors

The Seminole males were described by contemporary US Soldiers such as Private Bemrose as more often than not over six feet tall and having generally strong lower bodies but weaker upper body strength (Bemrose, 17). This may be attributed to the limited manual labor of their culture undertaken by the males coupled with their propensity for roaming across the lands on the hunt while domestic labor was handled by the women and the younger children.

They wore animal skin moccasins and would paint their bodies red and black for war, some wore jewels and feathery finery as distinctions. Others would wear clothing, such as jackets, taken from killed Soldiers or settlers to add to their native clothing while many were known to go to war nude or with only a loin cloth. The age of combatants would run from the late teens to those still capable of fighting. They voted with their feet and were only loosely controlled by their chiefs, mostly through cajoling and example more than anything else.

The warriors who fought Dade were all dismounted. A mounted element of Seminoles were present but were not involved in the fighting. The Seminoles throughout the war did not utilize the limited number of horses they had in a traditional mounted combat cavalry role but rather as a means of transportation and for the traditional scouting role of mounted forces. There are a few possibilities explaining the Seminole lack of horses in direct mounted combat. The lack of numbers of horses could be one, a result of inability to logistically support multiple horses on a campaign or the terrain not being conducive to mounted operations. This was supported by the US Army's relative light use of horses in direct combat action during the war. In addition, culturally, the Seminole livelihood did not place the same prominence on horses as did the Americans with their European background.

At the battle along Fort King Road, Micanopy's subordinate war chiefs were a youthful but experienced and competent pair. Alligator and Jumper were Micanopy's immediate subordinate leaders as Osceola would not be present due to his mission against the US Indian Affairs Agent Wiley Thompson.

Weapons

Projectile Weapons

For projectile weapons, the Seminoles relied almost exclusively on rifles. Contemporary US military participants recorded that the Spanish-made and imported rifle largely used by the Seminoles was even superior to the available US Army models. The Spanish rifles were small-bored and came from Cuba (Potter, Woodburne. *The War in Florida*. Baltimore, MD: Lewis and Coleman. 1836, 147). These Spanish rifles fired even a smaller caliber round than the Hall's model rifle which fired a .52 caliber round. As the war progressed, Soldiers' accounts would note the Seminoles had difficulty at times making these smaller caliber rounds effective at distance. This in some part giving credence to the previously noted US Army Soldiers' disparaging claims of the effectiveness of his available breech-loading Hall's rifle round which was of an even larger caliber than the Seminole's ammunition. Some US Army veterans of the war would later claim that the enemy fire was ineffective beyond 20 yards (Bemrose, 52-53). There remain questions if this was from lack of marksmanship and fire discipline or from an inferior weapon system. Nearly all the Seminoles were armed with rifles, some with acquired US weapons. In addition, the Seminoles lacked any form of artillery.

The rifles were not the only projectile weapons at the disposal of the Seminoles. They also utilized bows and arrows as well. The arrows were made from sugar cane stalks and were four feet long with pointed fiber tips. These tips were hardened through fire or at times shards of metal were used for the tips. The Seminoles, however, as a culture did not possess the knowledge for metal working and thus they could not make or repair their own rifles when these malfunctioned or broke. They relied on traders and settlers for all their metalworking needs, which of course, ceased when hostilities broke out.

Edged Weapons

The Seminoles possessed a variety of traditional "Indian" close-combat weaponry. They carried hunting knives, or scalping knives, as well as hatchets and clubs. These were crude instruments due to the lack of metal-working development in the Seminole culture at the time. The resulting reliance on settlers' metal-working abilities limited the quantity and quality of these sorts of weapons in comparison to those of the US Army's bayonets, swords, and axes. This was not a significant detriment to the Seminole fighting effort, however, as their tactics notably avoided close contact with Army Soldiers and rarely did fighting devolve to close quarter combat. These weapons were largely ceremonial in importance being used most commonly for post-combat actions such as scalp-taking or execution of wounded or prisoners of the enemy.

Tactics

"Indian" Fighting

The Seminoles would gather the necessary warriors from their scattered and loosely aligned clans to a centralized meeting place, usually at the warrior chief's camp. As the last red sticks signifying the countdown to the conflict were gathered up, the assembled warriors would be secluded for three days for purification ritual. Once this was complete the Seminole warriors would move out in single file, moving in the previous Seminole's footprints with the last Seminole in the order of movement covering the trail with grass. Whenever they stopped, they would circle with weapons outwards and the warrior chief controlling the one opening of the circle. He would use hand and arm signals to signal the others when to sleep and when to rise before they would commence their attack.

The tactics of the Seminole were that after the coordinated first volley, the battle became more of an individual fight or small groups controlled by a close leader. The tactics most employed, as recalled by US Army veterans, was for the Seminole to fire from the ground or a low crouch. After firing, they would let out a Seminole war-whoop and then fall or roll to the left to free up the right side for reloading the rifle. Consequently, a standard practice later developed by the US infantry was to fire to the right of where they saw the muzzle blasts. If this tactic, which was recognized during the later battles of the Second Seminole War, was true and accurate and perhaps displayed in the fight with Dade's men, then the relevant importance of the underbrush concealment and scattered trees of the battlefield take on more meaning.

Typically, once the initial fighting commenced, the Seminoles engaged in individual fights. However, the overall tendency in multiple engagements during the war was for the Seminoles to attempt to envelop the flanks of the US Soldiers. When the Seminoles were the defenders they tended to engage individually as they attempted to disengage from the contact.

Seminole marksmanship was brought into question by the US veterans. In many of the battles with the Seminoles, the first volley of the Seminoles was always said to be the most destructive. This is not unusual. In most militaries the opening salvo is the most accurate simply because it is loosed under the least pressure and with the most time and preparation.

This was the case with the Seminoles as well. The first volley was said to be extremely accurate, some argued that they even targeted officers in this volley. The follow up volleys were too hurried many observers commented, as if they fought in an ill-disciplined passion. US veteran reports recounted that after the battle, branches as high as 20 to 30 feet overhead were cut and broken from the Seminoles' wild rifle fire. Some reports even told of Seminoles missing their targets at four yards (Mahon, 120). It would not be unusual for these reports to be somewhat exaggerated as they mostly came from American sources but they may be grounded in a generalized truth.

In the fight with Dade's men, the Seminoles fought according to their standard methods. They fired a coordinated initial volley and then the fight devolved into many individual firefights among a dispersed Seminole formation against a scattered US force. As the battle developed, led in small groups, the Seminoles began to encroach on and then envelop the US position once the US Soldiers began to reconsolidate and reorganize into a static defensive position. Dade's battle was in fact one of the Seminole's most effective displays of this common tactic.

The effectiveness, if not professionalism, of the Seminoles should not be judged or questioned on this. Reference the skill sets supposedly possessed by the chief, Alligator, and the successfulness of the Seminoles at defying the US Army for so long and this cannot be disregarded easily.

Seminole Combat Support and Service Support Capabilities

Overview

Little is known regarding the combat support and service support capabilities of the Seminoles in regard to war-fighting. The Seminole support infrastructure was limited or nonexistent for protracted engagement, which explains their predilection towards smaller hit-and-run type engagements. Only if forced through US Army maneuver would they fight anything reflecting a set-piece battle. On only a few occasions did the US Army manage to maneuver into a place that forced the Seminoles to stand and fight in large numbers. When the Army managed to draw the Seminoles into a European-traditional battle it was always in vicinity of a major Seminole hamlet before the Seminoles had time to move their families and belongings and then it was only a delaying action until the families and provisions were either moved or destroyed. In any case, the lack of sustained infrastructure is the major factor influencing each of the following sections of Seminole support and service support categories.

Logistical Support

A military logistical system did not exist for the Seminole warriors. What they carried with them is what supported them. The Seminole logistical plan was only for the opening move and did not include contingencies for extended operations or re-supply. The Seminoles would declare intention for another fight by the distribution of red sticks, one stick equaling a day. The collection of sticks would be placed at the meeting lodges of the surrounding lesser tribes to signify the need for military provisions and volunteers for the coming fight with an appointed warrior chief's hamlet being the final gathering point. With a daily countdown removal of a red stick, the Seminoles knew when they would need to gather all they could provide to include manpower, logistical support, and sustainment to the warrior chief at the appointed collection point.

Though the Seminoles did not have a coordinated military strategy that envisioned or required prolonged support away from their tribal hamlets, this was not a detriment due to the cultural attitude from which the Seminoles approached warfare. The Seminoles were a mixed agricultural and hunting society. Their approach to a "war party" was an adaption to their hunting of deer and other animals to that of hunting man. They did not travel far from their hamlets to ambush or raid US Army patrols or settlements, usually returning home at the conclusion of the engagements. The few times they undertook a prolonged fight was in the vicinity of one of their larger hamlets where they lived and that was only long enough to get the women and children moved. This was only in the rare instances when the US Army surprised them.

The Seminole warriors' baggage train was their families' belongings as they eluded US Army patrols or if stationary, the warriors simply used their hamlets as a base of operations. Seminole logistics were labor-based. Old men and boys would carry powder in bags to the gathering place prior to the fight. Likewise, the women would cook extra food and bring it and bags of bullets to the meeting place signified by the collection of red sticks.

A major source of Seminole logistical movement was their canoes which utilized the many meandering waterways through the swamplands of Florida. These canoes were made of cypress tree trunks and could hold an estimated 20-30 warriors. These canoes and the attendant waterways were certainly a major means of transport of supplies for the Seminole Nation especially once war broke out. Trade with Cuba and the Bahamas was even recorded by Seminoles in these large canoes. This canoe transportation system gained more importance as the war progressed beyond Dade's Battle as the Seminoles began to embrace the necessary nomadic lifestyle required to avoid the US Army patrols and their attacks on Seminole hamlets. The Seminoles focused planting their agriculture, such as corn, on river banks to facilitate quiet and speedy gathering of these provisions by canoe. They would also began to bind the feet of their chickens and hogs to keep them from wandering too far in order to ease collection as well.

In addition, the Seminoles relied heavily on scavenging the battlefield after a fight for weapons, ammunition, and clothing to sustain them. Immediately before the outbreak of hostilities, Indian Affairs Agent Wiley Thompson outlawed the sale of weapons, powder, or bullets to the Seminoles. The later influx of US Army and US Navy forces into the territory greatly hampered any trading with the Seminoles which were confined to the interior of the peninsula with the Spanish and with bloodshed, even illicit trading between settlers and Seminoles was terminated. The Seminoles would be forced to mix rifle and musket powders as the majority of their rifle stores were exhausted in the opening fights and most of the plunder from battlefields with the US Army only resulted in musket supplies. By the end of the war, the Seminoles were relegated to handcrafting bullets from sheets of lead. However, for the opening confrontation of Dade's Battle, the Seminoles were at their peak of supplies due to ability for trading between settlers and Seminoles prior to hostilities. Exact numbers for the Seminole stores prior to and during the war are illusive due to the nature of Seminole historical record-keeping. They expected that by launching such a violent and stunning attack to terrorize the United States, that it would not be a long war.

By the illusive nature of the conflict and the terrain, the Seminoles operated on interior lines of communication as well as logistics. The inherent dispersed and defensive nature of their operations meant that they were not seriously hampered by their lack of organized combat support systems. They merely wanted to remain on their lands and it was up to the US Army to force them out. By necessity they lived and traveled light.

Engineer Support

The Seminoles had no training or professional understanding of engineer support for military operations. However, the Seminoles had an instinctual understanding of mobility and counter-mobility on the battlefield and in many cases applied this terrain analysis and understanding to tactical use. Though there was no Seminole engineer detachment or engineer branch, they still conducted operations that would be considered engineer-type operations in more organized and professional armies such as their counter-mobility operations against Dade's men when they burned the bridges over the swollen rivers. This both delayed the Soldiers as well as tired them by forcing them to ford the rivers and bring the cannon with them through manual labor and wagon across the waters. In addition, they made use as a people of the hammocks, hill-like protrusions from the otherwise mucky swamp-land. They made their homes on these hammocks and set up many of their ambushes on the pursuing or patrolling US Army Soldiers throughout the war.

Communications

The Seminole communications were at an organizational disadvantage to even the limited measures available to the US Army in that few could read or write in any language and that the Seminole language itself did not have a recognized written form. They still could pass information through personal messenger and this was certainly their primary measure to communicate. Since they resided in the interior of the peninsula they did not require large merchant ships for logistics or for communication, though they did possess smaller canoe-type craft for river navigation and communication in the swamps.

Medical

There is a distinctly limited knowledge of military medicine as practiced by the Seminoles. In fact, the medical knowledge of the Seminoles as a whole is sparse and non-specific. What is recorded is pre-battle purification ritual that lasted three days where the gathered warriors were secluded from the rest of the people and drank "war medicine" consisting of a brew of herbs and roots. The purpose of this was to purge the body and cleanse it before the fight but it also had the benefit to keep the warriors from drinking alcohol for three days before the fight. It is also thought that the Seminole disposition to fight in the near nude was a means to keep the clothing from causing infection by entering the wound if the Seminole was shot, though this is speculation.

Battlefield medicine for the Seminoles was basic as well. Each war party was to include a religious and medicinal participant, who refrained from entering the fight but stood away, praying for the warriors and providing rudimentary treatment to the wounded. This medicine man would carry a bag containing heads of parsley and when an injured Seminole was brought to him he would bite into the plant and apply it to the wound.

Intelligence

The Seminole intelligence "network" was a simple collection of rumor and sympathetic reports and observations. The Seminoles would receive information on troop movements, disposition, and activities from inside forts through African-American slaves sympathetic to the Seminole defense and of runaways and freed African-Americans. By the nature of the war, the Seminoles lived around the forts and had regular interaction with the Soldiers and settlers, both friend and foe, and through this they gained critical intelligence and insight into the US Army and the citizens. Prior to the outbreak of hostilities, a Seminole chief stated they had been planning the opening attack for nearly a year before it happened, just waiting for an opportunity to present itself, which it did with Dade's march. Private Bemrose noted in his writings on seeing Seminoles watching closely the US Soldiers' drilling and marksmanship training (Bemrose, 25). Through a combination of sympathetic reporting from the slaves, direct observation through reconnaissance by Seminoles themselves, and an inherent knowledge of the land, the Seminoles gathered significant knowledge to greatly influence their chances for success in ambushes and raids or successfully evade if outmatched.

Part II. Dade's Campaign Overview

Introduction

On the 28 December in 1835 deteriorating relations between the US Government and the Seminole Nation in the territory of Florida escalated into outright hostility. This was not the first time that violence had been undertaken to resolve disputes in Florida over expanding grasp on the continent nor would it be the last. On that day Seminole chieftain Osceola and his culturally superior Chief Micanopy executed a two-pronged aggressive operation meant to persuade and intimidate (through violence) Washington and the local settlers of Florida into simply leaving the Seminoles alone.

Osceola lay in wait to ambush the official government representative to the Seminoles, Indian Affairs Agent Wiley Thompson and his dinner guests. Meanwhile, Micanopy and a few hundred warriors lay in wait along the Fort King Road to engage a contingent of US Army Regulars under the command of Brevet Major Francis Dade. Dade's command was marching through the declared Seminole Nation under direct orders to reinforce the commander of the US forces in Florida, Brevet Brigadier General Duncan Clinch, in preparation for military operations to persuade and intimidate the Seminole Nation into leaving their homes in accordance with a series of treaties.

Morning of the 29th December, 1835 would find the political power of Washington questioned with the murder of Agent Thompson by Osceola while likewise the military might of the young US Army was tested with the isolated and final stand of Dade's command on a long and lonely road. With these twin attacks, the Seminole Nation ushered in the long and bloody Second Seminole War, also known at the time as "the Florida War".

The Drums of War

There were two arguably intertwined political reasons for the aggressive posture that the United States was taking with the "Indian question" concerning the Seminoles of Florida. First it was an issue of slavery and second the expansion of American settlers across the peninsula. By 1835, the Seminole Nation had voluntarily confined themselves to a "nation" that encompassed the interior of the peninsula, providing the United States willingly with the Florida Panhandle and the coastlines. However, the Seminole practice of openly accepting runaway slaves into their society as equals coupled with the growing desire to connect the coastlines, for commercial reasons, set the Seminoles and the local white settlers on a collision course and thus pulled the United States into the contentious issue of further Seminole restrictions.

A series of three treaties in regard to the fate of the Seminole tribes, defined the political climate that initiated the series of events culminating in the fateful order for the march of a token US force through the heart of the Seminole Nation. These three treaties set the political and diplomatic climate for the outbreak of hostilities with each following Washington's overall Indian removal policy.

The first treaty, the Treaty of Moultrie Creek of 1823, established the reservation in the heart of Florida as the Seminole Nation. This reservation was 60 miles by 120 miles. This treaty further tasked the US government to control unwanted trespassing of whites into the Seminole Nation and likewise made the Seminole chiefs responsible for the monitoring and controlling of Seminole traffic outside of the reservation.

The Treaty of Payne's Landing of 1832 was the next diplomatic agreement following the Treaty of Moultrie Creek. The critical provision of this treaty was for the transportation of Seminole chiefs to see the proposed lands west of the Mississippi River to which they were to be transferred and where, upon approval, would be sent. Discrepancies in the text of this treaty would cloud this matter in history. A question of whose approval was binding–that of only the chiefs who would speak for the nation or the nation's approval to what the chiefs would return to propose to them. The US Government saw the chiefs as the representatives of the people, thus their decision was binding. However, some Seminole chiefs, the later war leaders, said they could only propose to the nation and the nation itself would have to choose. In the end, a direct result of the Treaty of Payne's Landing was the final treaty leading to the Second Seminole War, the Treaty of Gibson in 1833. This treaty came about after Seminole Chiefs travelled to the lands upon which they were to be relocated and gave their tacit approval for the movement of the tribe. However, the US Government never really understood that the Seminole Nation was not a unified political entity and thus many Seminoles rejected the treaty and refused to relocate. The treaty provided the US government with political capital to use military force to compel the resisting Seminoles to "honor" their agreement to transfer from Florida to the lands west of the Mississippi in the Arkansas and Oklahoma territories.

As a result of the diplomatic pressure of the political treaties culminating in the Treaty of Gibson, the military climate of Florida led to a sharp divide among the Seminole tribes. This divide led to a growing violence among smaller groups of the Seminoles and both the encroaching settlers and their United States Army defenders.

There were a variety of depredations committed leading up to the battle of Major Dade's command. There was a brief skirmish between settlers and a Seminole warrior party at Hog Town after the locals reportedly caught some Seminoles stealing. There was a brief exchange of small arms fire, and then the settlers tied up and flogged a captured "thief." Due to the sensitive cultural nature of Seminole's regard for personal honor and revenge for affronts, the second notable violent act occurred. Tacitly, in response to the humiliation and abuse of the flogging of the Seminole, a group of Seminoles vowed revenge. This revenge was executed on a solitary US Soldier serving as a courier between Fort Brooke on Tampa Bay and the main post of Fort King northeast along the Fort King Road. The unfortunate soldier was Private Kinsley Dalton. Private Dalton was found scalped and disemboweled on the side of the road with the dispatches he was carrying scattered about the road. As the escalation rose, it was not limited only to Seminole against United States but even amongst Seminoles themselves. A prominent Seminole chief, Omathla also known as "Charley," was murdered in front of his family by Osceola, a growing dissenter championing war. Omathla was targeted after having sold his cattle in preparation to follow up with his pronounced position to relocate and leave Florida to the encroaching whites. This would serve to intimidate Seminoles, radicalize dissenters and advance the young Osceola's standing among the warriors.

The final escalation toward war was a skirmish prior to the march of Dade's command where a raid was conducted by a Seminole war party on a government supply train. This skirmish fought on 18 December 1835, known by some at the time as the "battle of Black Point," resulted in six wounded and two dead US and a loss of two wagons burned but with Seminole losses unknown.

This developing whirlwind of increasing violence resulted in Brigadier General Clinch's plan to use military force to influence Seminole cooperation. Under pressure from Washington to enforce the treaty stipulations and the local Floridians' calls for an end to the violence, Clinch sought to gather his available forces together and then to move on the larger Seminole homesteads.

Orders to March

On the 16 December in 1835, General Clinch sent orders to the commandant of Fort Brooke to send two companies of Regulars to link up with his assembled forces at Fort King near the Withlacoochie River. It was Captain Francis S. Belton who, as acting commandant, received

General Clinch's orders. The guidance received was to send the available two companies, which were Captain George Washington Gardiner's C Company, 2d Artillery Regiment and Captain Upton Fraser's B Company, 3d Artillery Regiment. After these two companies were sent, the other two inbound from Key West were to follow.

Captain Belton deferred as long as he could for the reinforcements from Key West to arrive. Belton struggled to comply with the orders from his superior. However, as fort commandant, he had to keep the safety of the fort in mind as well as that of the civilians who had flocked to the fort during the growing violence. Also, as any professional soldier would, Belton preferred to wait for the entire reinforcement contingent to arrive so that four companies could be sent together through "Indian country" as the road to Fort King and the Withlacoochie from Fort Brooke went right through the heart of the Seminole Nation. However, General Clinch ordered reinforcements, with all haste, as soon as they were readied.

Belton, in the age of slow courier-driven communications, had no way of knowing the exact circumstances of Fort King, though he did know the circumstances of Fort Brooke intimately as acting commandant. Equally so, General Clinch couldn't know of the exact circumstances of Fort Brooke. General Clinch's entire command in Florida was of 700 Regulars with a recently added muster of 150 militia "horse" or mounted infantry. This was due to the "shallow opinion…of the Seminoles" held by those in command and distant from the immediate violence. Recently, it could be heard from one Captain Gustavus Drane that he could take his entire 60-man command through the Seminole Nation unscathed. Some were aware of the dangers and abilities of the Seminole, others were not, but some would be vindicated while others humbled in the coming days (Bemrose, 32).

As Captain Belton wrestled with the decision of when to commence Captains Gardiner and Fraser and their companies on the march, a ship from Key West arrived. On it was B Company from the 4th Infantry Regiment under Major Francis Dade. Using the infantrymen from Major Dade's detachment to round out the Artillery companies, Captain Belton decided he must follow orders. Against his own judgment, he ordered the march to commence on the 23rd of December, at dawn.

Each company had been bolstered to 50 "bayonets" (referring to enlisted men), plus seven officers and an attached medical officer, Assistant Surgeon Dr. John Gatlin. Captain Belton had also contracted the service of both a Seminole and an African-American translator to accompany the march. Though Captain Fraser was senior in captaincy to Captain Gardiner by a number of years, he gave command to Gardiner in light of Gardiner's West Point appointment whereas Fraser was promoted from the ranks. It was at this point as the contingent was preparing to depart that Major Dade spoke up on behalf of a troubled but dutiful Captain Gardiner. Captain Gardiner's wife was extremely ill at Fort Brooke's infirmary. Major Dade offered to Captain Belton to lead the march in place of Gardiner to allow Gardiner to stay with his wife. Captain Belton acquiesced and that morning, Major Dade led the column out the gates of Fort Brooke and onto the road to Fort King while Captain Gardiner returned to his ill wife's side. It was a momentous decision for Major Dade. Under no obligation to take part on a certainly dangerous mission, Major Dade offered his services to allow a fellow officer to remain with his sick wife. Before they left, Major Dade made it of utmost importance to take a cannon with them. Belton was able to assist them with one 6-pounder field piece, drawn by four oxen. This would be of critical importance in the coming battle.

Even with Major Dade's selfless act of taking charge from Captain Gardiner to allow Gardiner to tend to personal affairs, fate would not leave Gardiner alone. On the second day of the march, news came to Fort Brooke that the oxen with the cannon had fallen behind and Major Dade requested Belton to do all he could to supply them the necessary team of draft horses to help the cannon retake the marching column. Simultaneously, a merchant schooner bound for Key West arrived and Captain Gardiner was able to secure passage on it for his ill wife to travel to Key West was immediate family resided that could care for her. Having his wife's affairs taken care of, Captain Gardiner stubbornly and devoutly loyal to his men would not see them through enemy territory and suffer privations that he did not as well. He requested, permission from Belton to rejoin the column. Belton granted it, and both Gardiner and the cannon retook the column that evening. Upon arrival, Gardiner explained securing his wife's departure to Key West thereby allowing him, "his earnest desire to be with his men" (Bemrose, 63). Seeing the situation as it was, Captain Gardiner acquiesced to Major Dade to maintain command of the column. Captain Gardiner only wanted to be restored to command of his C Company, 2d Artillery.

The March

The contingent departed Fort Brooke on the 23d of December and began their 125 mile march along the Fort King Road. They marched in two man columns with an advance guard and main body accompanying the cannon and wagon and a rear guard. Dade had pushed out flankers to the sides each day along the march. Under orders, they established breastworks of timber and logs at night for their bivouacs along with sentries and camp fires. Private Clark recalled hearing Seminoles every night from departure of Fort Brooke trailing them. At night they would hear Seminoles calling out and moving around but never saw any. The cannon and wagon slowed the rate of march and when they came across the river crossings such as the Hillsborough River, and later the most dangerous portion the Soldiers thought the Withlacoochie swampland, the cannon was an abysmal accompaniment. The bridges had been burned. This was assumed by the Soldiers to be the work of Seminoles but never proven. The Soldiers did not really care, all they knew is in the frigid winter weather they had to attach harness and ropes and haul the cannon through the river and up the embankments each time which was exhausting work. In fact, one soldier was so injured by this work that he was sent back, alone, to Fort Brooke due to his injuries. He did not report any assaults by Seminoles on him, they let him go. They were focused on Dade and the main force moving down the road. Likewise, by this time, the Seminole guide and all other civilians were gone save one Louis Pacheo who was the lone remaining translator and African-American slave.

Dawn broke on the 28th of December. The troops were judged to be within one day's movement from Fort King. The journey was almost over without Seminole assault and now the terrain was opening up, vegetation was thinning, and the Soldiers could see further. The air was damp from the previous evening's light rain. Rain had been plaguing them all along the march adding to the coolness of the average 70s to 50s Fahrenheit. As they moved north along Fort King Road, Major Dade promised the men, "I'll give you three days for Christmas! Have a good heart, difficulties and dangers now over." (Laumer, 179). This brought a cheer from among the men. As they moved down, nearing their objective, perhaps a false sense of security set over them because Dade did not order out skirmishers even as the land opened up. The claim was that the mounted force or those on the wagon could see farther than a skirmisher in the underbrush and that the underbrush would slow down the skirmishers and thus the entire command when they were so close. Major Dade kept all his command close and in marching order along the road. This was not the only instance of a lackadaisical approach to forced marches during this period in Florida. There were similar records of march with no scouts, no pickets, and arms unloaded until 50 miles into the march. The weather being cold, the march having started at dawn and it now between 0800 and 0900, the Soldiers had marched for roughly four hours already that morning. Major Dade allowed the men to button their overcoats over their shouldered arms in addition to their cartridge boxes and ammunition sacks to keep warm and keep the dampness out.

When they approached the Seminole positions, the US Army was organized in an advance guard of six enlisted men under the command of Second Lieutenant Robert Mudge. He was joined by Captain Fraser, Major Dade, and the translator Pacheo. This detachment led the main column by 200 yards and walked in single file. The main force followed in two-man columns led by Captain Gardiner with the wagon and cannon trailing this formation and directly in front of the rear guard under the charge of Second Lieutenant William Bassinger.

The Ambush

The Seminoles waited in ambush ahead in moccasins and skins, some in feathers and finery and many painted in blacks and reds. As they lay in the tall grass spread out along the west and north of the approaching US Army Soldiers with a pond bordering the east of the road, they waited to implement a plan that was supposedly a year in the making. The plan was two-pronged to deliver both a political strike and a military intimidation. They were to kill the Indian Affairs Agent while simultaneously striking a military blow by knocking out a vulnerable military unit, Dade's command. Osceola said that Agent Thompson was "his friend, he would see to him" (Sprague, 90). Earlier, Agent Thompson had placed Osceola in chains for an unrecorded outrage and had forever darkened Osceola's relations towards him. Osceola did what was necessary to be released and seem Thompson's friend but merely waited to exact his revenge for his tainted honor.

Private Bemrose commented that he had observed the Seminoles watching the Soldiers train at Fort King previously, including the Soldiers' "woodland drill" to "fight like the Indians" as well as the Soldiers' marksmanship (Bemrose, 25). The strained relationship between African-Americans and the United States in Florida due to slavery and race relations concerning the Seminole assistance did not help matters as claims were made of treachery by African-Americans running ahead and telling the Seminoles of the number of Dade's command and their departure. Some even claim that Pacheo was a traitor as well, who at this point was Dade's only Seminole-speaker.

Even at the most modest accounts, the Seminoles had assembled a few hundred warriors to meet Dade's command. There were even reports of upwards of one hundred mounted Seminoles present. The site chosen was not the first choice. The original intention had been to attack the Soldiers three days earlier, but the gathered Seminoles were without major tribal leadership at that time, neither Micanopy or Osceola were present. When

Micanopy arrived, he had argued for delay until Osceola could join but Osceola would not, as he was intent to strike at Agent Thompson. Jumper, one of Micanopy's junior assisting war chiefs with Alligator, chastised Micanopy's lack of initiative and was worried the favorable time would pass. Jumper addressed those present and told those who were faint hearted to remain behind but he would go forward. He called Micanopy out in front of the assembled warriors and Micanopy agreed to go forward with the ambush of Dade's men.

They chose the site as the last favorable location before the Soldiers would be too close to Fort King and also too far from the swampland. The swamps were the unchallenged territory of the Seminoles. They knew it well and they knew the Soldiers could not effectively operate in it. They lay in the tall grass no more than 30 yards from the edge of the road as the advance guard approached, followed by the rest of the column.

Up until the last possible moment, Micanopy is said to have hesitated until his two subordinate chiefs and known warriors, Jumper and Alligator, told him in no uncertain terms that he was either with them or against them. To this, Micanopy reportedly replied, "I will show you." (George A. McCall, *Letters from the Frontiers,* Philadelphia, PA: J.B. Lippincott and Company, 1868, 303-304). Micanopy rose and as per the signal for the first volley, fired. He shot the mounted Major Dade. The postmortem wound would indicate that he was shot through the heart. Micanopy said he knew Dade from when he had befriended him in Tampa and it would be he who would kill him. Strikingly similar to what Osceola said concerning his personal targeting of Agent Thompson.

Accounts differ slightly on the time of the first volley but it is certainly between 0800 and 0900. Clark said he distinctly heard a single first shot and before he or anyone could react to it there came fire "as if from a thousand rifles" along the entire formation from forward (the north) and from the left (the west) (Account of Ransom Clark, as reprinted in Laumer, 236). The first volley was highly destructive, taking out half of all the Soldiers. The entire advance guard was killed immediately as their bodies were found where they fell right in the road in marching order with the exception of Captain Fraser who had crawled a little ways to lean against a tree on the side of the road before dying and Second Lieutenant Mudge who would crawl back to the main force and die alongside them. Brevet Second Lieutenant John Keyes had both his arms broken in the first volley and unresponsively sat out the rest of the battle until he was killed where he leaned against a tree. Another lieutenant, Richard Henderson, was shot through the arm in the initial volley with the main body.

The Seminoles would have fired, let out a war-whoop starting as a guttural growl and ending in a high-pitched yell, adding to the din of the combat after each time they fired. As was described by one Seminole War veteran, "the crack of rifles was one incessant peal of sharp... bells to which the loud report of musketry and the booming of the artillery formed a fitting, though fearful accompaniment." (McCall, 305). In addition, it was reported that over the woods ringing with war-whoops, could be heard Captain Gardiner's boisterous commands.

Private Clark wrote that for the first seven or more volleys from the woods, he did not even see a Seminole. When he did start seeing them, he fired only at identified targets and these were merely heads and shoulders which was all he could see in the tall grass or around trees.

When the first assault turned into a regular engagement, the Seminoles fought in widely scattered groups in a semi-circle covering west to north. The pond was on the east and to the south was the road back to dense vegetation. The mounted Seminoles remained aloof from the fighting, arrayed to the north to cut off any fleeing Soldiers towards Fort King.

It can be imagined that the Soldiers were exhausted and sore from five days of marching and fording rivers with the cannon. They were cold and shivering from the drizzling rain and winter weather and had psychologically lowered their guard as well as physically and were stunned in the initial moments of the ambush. Half of their forces were knocked out with half of the officers, including their commander, killed immediately. Having come so far to Fort King to be attacked now with the entire advance guard wiped out and no word or sign from them and only 200 yards away, must have been demoralizing. They must have struggled to unbutton overcoats in order to bring muskets to bear, rifling through cartridge sacks if a red-legged infantryman or a cartridge box if one of the few true-blue infantrymen. The immediate cacophony of Seminole whooping, the rifle and soon musket fire and the cries of wounded and bellowing commands of Captain Gardiner, made for a shocking departure from the seconds previous silence. Soon the cannon was unlimbered and added its booming to the fight under the command of Lieutenant Bassinger as directed by Captain Gardiner.

The Soldiers Rally

The Soldiers dispersed to fight as light infantry, each behind a tree returning individual fire. This would not be a linear rank-and-file coordinated volley battle by the seriously reduced US Army forces. The Seminoles were firing in the manner that later veterans of the Seminole

War would recognize, at a crouch from behind a tree or on the ground. Lieutenant Bassinger placed the six-pounder into action, firing grapeshot in the general direction of the Seminole fire. The men who manned the cannon were shot down as soon as the smoke cleared from the last round fired. Seminole accounts mention their specific targeting of the artillerymen around the cannon as does the narrative of the surviving US soldier, Private Clark (Sprague, 91 and Account of Ransom Clark, as reprinted in Laumer, 236). Mixed with the grapeshot were solid shots, however, these solid shot cannon balls soared over the heads of the Seminoles, most likely due to the immediacy of the cannon's utilization, giving the artillerymen no time to lay aiming lines or judge distance but just immediately putting it to work. The booming certainly had an effect, even if the solid shot went over the Seminoles' heads. The artillerymen were at their best manning the six-pounder while others along with the infantrymen kept up a musketry fire. As one artilleryman at the cannon fell, another took his place. The cannon's position was the most exposed with Lieutenant Bassinger by its side directing its fire while Captain Gardiner rallied the scattered men. The grapeshot fire from the cannon, the small containers full of small balls meant to spread out like a shotgun blast, was certainly more effective against the scattered Seminoles. By the time the Seminoles began to fall back from the road, the cannon reportedly fired five to six rounds.

After about an hour of fighting the Seminoles had enough of the cannon and the stubborn fire of the remaining bluecoats and fell back about a half a mile, having fired 12 to 15 volleys from Private Clark's account (Account of Ransom Clark, as reprinted in Laumer, 236). The cannon had bought the small band of Army Regulars a respite.

Captain Gardiner did not waste a minute of this respite. He ordered the scattered wounded to be brought to the cannon's position where others were ordered to begin felling some young trees to make a hasty breastwork, a logged redoubt anchored by the cannon. Others began scrounging among the dead and wounded for more ammunition. The breastworks were formed into interlocking layers making a triangle. These breastworks were about two and a half feet tall. There were barely over 30 Soldiers left at this point as Captain Gardiner organized a last stand defense. His defense was based around the cannon, which anchored the north point of the redoubt. The Soldiers manned the west and north legs of the triangle works as the east faced the pond and they took no fire from Seminoles from that direction. The wounded were brought into the works and Dr. Gatlin did what he could, but the hard-won respite would not last long.

Gardiner decided he had no choice but to stay. The wounded had no transport, the cannon which was what was keeping the Seminoles at bay, was not maneuverable in the least and the only way back was a long multi-day retreat to Fort Brooke. He determined they could not break out towards Fort King and could not survive if they dispersed in the open area and in view of mounted Seminoles. No, they had to stay and fight with the wounded and the cannon. Maybe, Gardiner thought, the Seminoles would retreat and leave the survivors alone and Gardiner, without immediate pressure, could find away to transport the wounded or at least get a runner to Fort King or back to Fort Brooke. A professional like Gardiner knew what he had to do, knew his duty to his men, and knew what had brought him here from his ill wife's side. They all would stay with the wounded and the cannon.

Final Assault

The Seminoles regrouped a half mile away from the Soldiers' final stand. There the chiefs received reports of the breastwork going up. Chiefs Jumper and Alligator sought to return to finish off the remaining Soldiers. The others, not mentioned but certainly including Micanopy, refused. It took derision and insults from the two warrior chiefs to get the Seminoles to go back, "asking them if they were drunk, sick or women to be afraid of a few white men." (M.M.Cohen, *Notices of Florida and the Campaigns*. Charleston, S.C.: Burges and Honour, 1836, 77).

In less than 45 minutes, the Soldiers saw the Seminoles begin advancing again. They were in open order until within range and once the cannon and the muskets began firing, the Seminoles scattered, moving and fighting from tree to tree to avoid the cannon fire. This diluted the deadly effect of the cannon fire but the cannon still roared. The Seminoles purposefully targeted the men manning the cannon in between the smoke from the firing. Bodies began to pile up alongside the gun as men worked over the fallen forms of their comrades to keep the cannon going. Alligator, in his sole Seminole account of the fighting, recalled that "The Soldiers shouted and whooped and the officers shook their swords and swore loudly." He distinctly recalled, "There was a little man, a great brave, who shook his sword at the Soldiers and said, 'god-dam!' no rifle-ball could hit him." (Sprague, 91). This likely was Captain Gardiner who stayed in the center of the works controlling the Soldiers while Second Lieutenant Bassinger manned the cannon. Wounded Second Lieutenant Henderson, with one good arm, fired from inside the works until it was felled by the Seminoles, firing a reported 30 to 40 rounds before dying.

The Seminoles began spreading out, forcing the few scattered Soldiers like Private Clark who had been skirmishing out behind trees into the breastworks. Clark claims to have shot three Seminoles alone, and fired 40 to 50 rounds never failing to properly identify his target (Account of Ransom Clark, as reprinted in Laumer, 237). No matter the effort made by the Soldiers, the Seminoles were closing the noose. The Soldiers kept up a brisk fire punctuated by the cannon. However, the cannon only had 50 rounds and fast expending them along with the growing casualties around, exposed its position.

At least the breastworks provided some measure of protection. The Soldiers killed in the redoubt were from shots to the head and neck and countless rifle balls were found lodged in the breastworks. Then Captain Gardiner, the "great brave" that "no rifle-ball could hit" was struck mortally. He fell in the center of the redoubt he had commanded constructed to protect his wounded men. He cried out, "I can give you no more orders, my lads, do your best." (Woodburne Potter, *The War in Florida*. Baltimore, MD: Lewis and Coleman, 1836, 105) Once Captain Gardiner died, the only remaining combat arms officer remaining was Lieutenant Bassinger and he was already wounded. He said, "I am the only officer left, boys. We must do the best we can." (Account of Ransom Clark, as reprinted in Laumer, 239). The cannon had fired 49 of its fifty rounds, the final round was loaded but went unfired. The Soldiers were out of ammunition. Dr. Gatlin leaning on the works with his double-barreled shotguns where he would die said, "Well, I have got four barrels for them!" (Account of Ransom Clark, as reprinted in Laumer, 239).

As the Seminoles approached for the final push with the now silent cannon and empty muskets, Lieutenant Bassinger, the only remaining officer, told Clark "to feign myself dead" (Sprague, 91) saving Clark's life. Clark claims the firing lasted from 0800 to 1400 with the 45 minute lull after the first hour of fighting. Before the approaching Seminole's entered, Clark recorded one short stout one give a short speech. This must have been Micanopy gloating over the dead Soldiers, as certainly the Seminoles upon their approach, figured there were no survivors. The Seminoles found no ammunition in any of the Soldiers' packs. One wounded soldier seized a Seminole's rifle, wrenched it from his hands and killed him with a blow to his head and then ran, only to be chased down by two mounted Seminoles, who perhaps afraid to face such a frenzied soldier, shot him from afar.

Clark recalled that the Seminoles did not desecrate the dead. They merely picked over the weapons and equipment and took scalps. However, once the Seminoles left a band of their African-American followers (about 50) they began looting and killing the remaining wounded. As they came, a Soldier tried to run but was shot by a Seminole from behind a tree. With the killing going on Lieutenant Bassinger, still alive, rose and offered his sword and pleaded for a stop to the killing. He was struck down.

The battle was over. Three Soldiers survived to try and make their way back to Fort Brooke, even though closer, none wanted to follow the departing Seminoles and their African-American partners north towards Fort King. Private Clark was wounded five times: in the right shoulder, in the right thigh, in the right temple, his back, and in an arm. He could not walk and had to crawl his way back to Fort Brooke. He started off with another survivor but on the first day on the road back to Fort Brooke, they came across a mounted Seminole and split up. The Seminole pursued the other survivor and killed him. Failing to find Clark, he left and Clark continued on alone. Three days later, Clark arrived at Fort Brooke and when treated for his wounds, was "swearing most terribly and continually whilst under the surgeon's hands… when any bones were removed… asking if they would make good soup." (Bemrose, 65).

Clark would later write an account of the battle and his ordeal. The other survivor, Private Joseph Sprague, left no written record after making it back on 1 January, 1836 to Fort Brooke. On 29 December, Private John Thomas, the one with the injured back from moving the cannon across the river, made it back to the fort with no knowledge of the fighting. Together, these three would be the only soldier survivors of Dade's command. The translator-slave Louis Pacheo survived the fight, was spared by the Seminoles and kept by them. It's not known whether this was willingly or not. Years after the fact, Pacheo would leave a written account of the fight as well. Together with Alligator's Seminole account, these three make up the only eye witness accounts of the battle.

Only three enlisted Soldiers survived of Major Dade's "bayonets", one of which was not even present at the fight. No officers lived but the one translator did, accounting for 105 US Army deaths. Of the Seminoles, Alligator's account claimed only three Seminoles were killed and five wounded, this low estimate interestingly matches the exact same report given by the Seminoles as their record of losses at another large-scale battle, that of the Battle of Withlacoochie which would take place only a few days later. When Osceola first heard the report of the attack on Dade's column he was informed that the Seminoles had killed 200 whites for a loss of 100 Seminoles and had captured "a big gun", fought "all day". (Cohen, 77). It had been a blood-red day (see Table Two).

Table Two:
Dade's Battle Casualties

	United States Army Present	United States Army Wounded	United States Army Killed	Seminole Nation Present	Seminole Nation Wounded	Seminole Nation Killed
Soldiers/ Warriors	100	2	98	200-500	5 (reported)	3-50 (reported)
Officers/ Chiefs	8	N/A	8	3	N/A	0
Total	108	2	106	203-503	UNK	UNK

The Aftermath

It would not be until 20 February 1836 that blue-clad Soldiers would see the site of Dade's last stand. These Regulars were from New Orleans under the command of General Edmund Pendleton Gaines coming to aid General Clinch. Though it had been nearly 60 days, the battlefield remained untouched, the Soldiers remained where they fell, aligned to the north and west facing their enemy, many in the road where they fell after the first volley, including the advance party. The first signs of struggle were seen 100 yards to the east of the works as the column approached. When they neared the incomplete breastworks one officer said, "The picture of those brave men lying thus in their 'sky-blue' clothing… was such as can never be effaced from my memory." (Sprague, 108). All the bodies in the breastworks were found kneeling or lying with their heads resting on the timbers. The fellow officers identified their fallen peers and friends. The fallen remained at right angles to the works, "as if they had been toy-Soldiers arranged by a child." (McCall, *Letters from the Frontiers*, 306)

Graves were dug and the remains were separated by rank of officers, NCOs, and enlisted. The cannon, retrieved from where it had been dumped in the nearby pond, was placed upside down on top of the officers' grave as what was seen to be a short-term memorial. The 4th Infantry Regimental Band of Major Dade's former unit, led the procession followed by the officer who had known the deceased and then in a two-man column, was the rest of General Gaines' command. They made three circuits around the small gravesite dug in the middle of where the interned had made their final stand and arms were reversed. Then it was over and the Army moved on to the dirty business of a new war.

Part III. Suggested Stands (Sites) to Visit
Introduction

The Dade Battle staff ride is composed of nine suggested stands to support a comprehensive study and analysis of the battle. However, to adjust for available time considerations and additional starting locations, a seven-stand option is available as well and is entirely contained at the site of the battlefield. The full nine suggested stands incorporate the entire march of Dade's command from the site of Fort Brooke on Tampa Bay (current site of the Cotanchobee/Fort Brooke Park) along modern US 301 (old Fort King Road), a stop addressing fording the Hillsborough River, and ending at the site of the battle. This involves additional driving compared to the seven-stand option but provides the most complete overview and experience of Dade's Battle. The seven-stand option involves one vehicular movement to the site of the battle. Once here, a simple overview of the campaign should be added to Stand three (the first stand on the actual battle site) with no other additional changes. By necessity, the seven-stand option removes certain operational aspects of the staff ride and lessens terrain analysis, specifically the river crossings and their entailed vulnerabilities.

Stand One

Fort Brooke and Decision to March: Overview

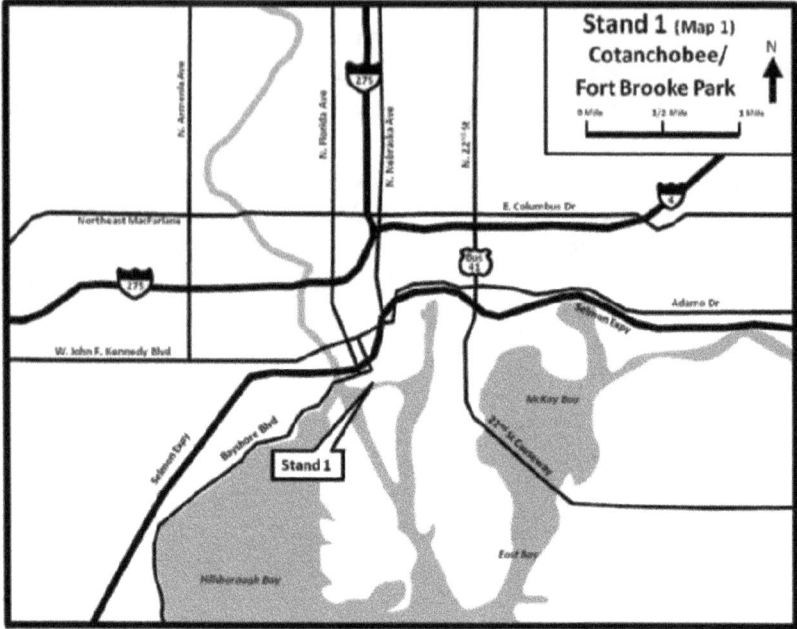

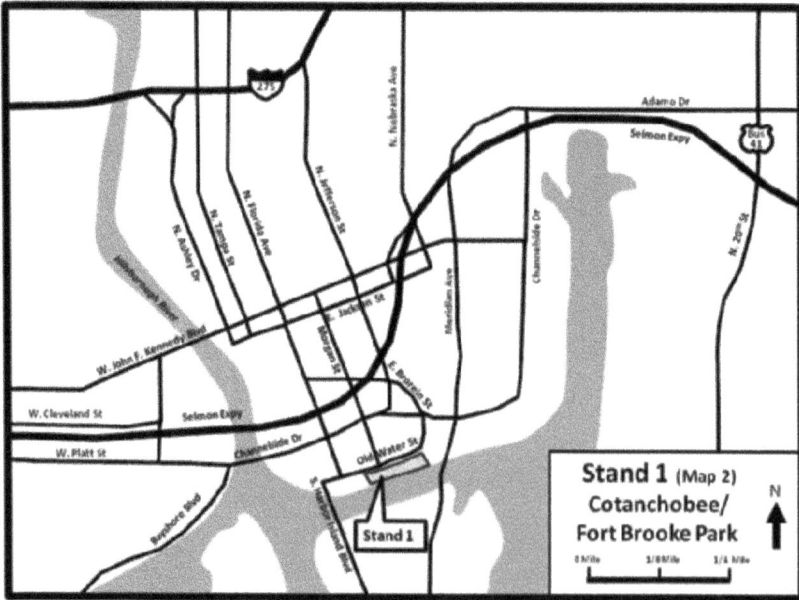

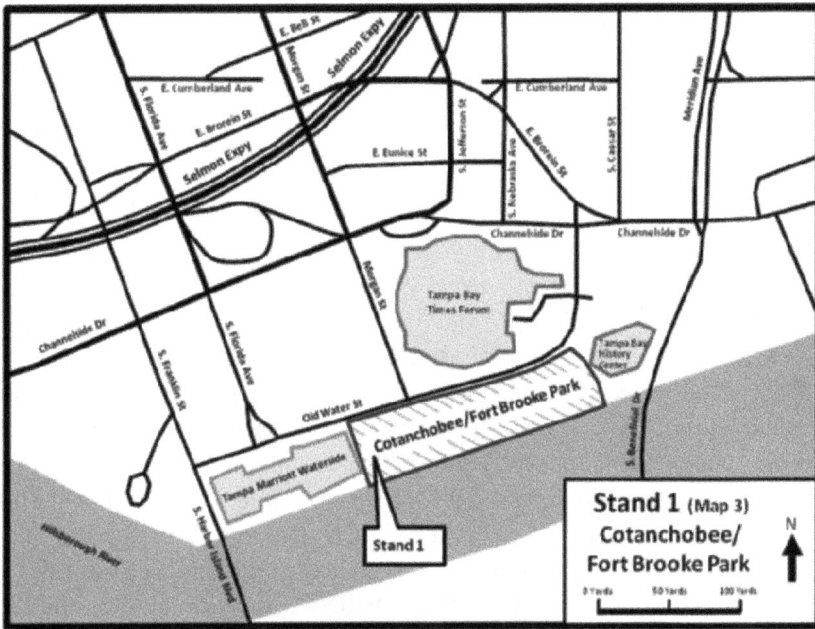

Directions: Stand One is at the Fort Brooke Plaque in the Cotanchobee/ Fort Brooke Park located at 801 Old Water Street, Tampa FL, 33602 near the site of the current Tampa Bay History Center. Both the Tampa Bay History Center and the nearby Tampa Marriot Waterside Hotel have areas for bus drop off. In addition, there is parking available at the historic center as well as across the street at the Tampa Bay Times Forum. On the west side of the park near the hotel, is a Fort Brooke Plaque in the walkway. Conduct the stand near the plaque.

Visual Aids: Historical Map 1: Fort Brooke, Historical Map 2: Area of Dade's March.

Orientation: The Cotanchobee/Fort Brooke Park runs along the Tampa Bay riverfront and between the Tampa Bay History Center and the Tampa Marriot Waterside Hotel. To the south is the waterway and to the east is a bridge to Harbor Island. Directly west of the plaque there is the Tampa Marriot Waterside Hotel and another bridge crossing the waterway. There are no remains of the original Fort Brooke at the site. In the 1830s, Fort Brooke comprised what is now the park along with the Tampa Bay History Center and the Tampa Marriot Waterside Hotel along the waterfront. The fort was composed of barracks for officers and enlisted personnel, a set of storehouses, livestock stables, a small hospital, a kitchen, and a guardhouse. The fort did not possess a palisade or defensive walls until there was an immediate threat and then palisades were cut and placed. These were removed once the threat had passed and stored until the threat returned when they were placed again. Likewise, when threatened, ditches were dug around the perimeter and stakes were placed in the ditches to keep attackers from the edges of the palisades. The ditches were filled with hay or straw to hide the stakes. Similar to the palisades, these defensive trenches were filled in and re-dug based on the perceived threat to the fort.

Description: The entire struggle of Major Dade's column with the Seminoles on the Fort King Road can be traced to Brigadier General Clinch's order to Fort Brooke's acting commandant, Captain Belton, to send to him four companies at Fort King. General Clinch's insistence that it was to be done with all due haste—two companies at a time since Fort Brooke had not received its second pair of companies yet—emphasized this need for speed. Due to the nature of the communications of the period, Brigadier General Clinch was in the dark as to the current situation at Fort Brooke and equally so was Captain Belton to that of Clinch at Fort King. With the growing hostility, the two forts had not communicated via courier for crucial weeks in which time relations between the Seminoles and the United States were deteriorating exponentially.

Brigadier General Clinch wanted the reinforcements, essentially his entire US Army Regulars, together for his proposed pre-emptive offensive to end the growing Seminole violence and resistance to the enforcement of the movement treaties. It is always far clearer to look in retrospection on critical decisions. With the information on hand, General Clinch knew he had growing physical discontent with the Seminoles and he wanted to strike at a center of gravity of the Seminoles, a large hamlet near the Withlacoochie, and doing so demanded that he concentrate his available means.

According to General Clinch's plan, with the reinforcements from Fort Brooke, his combined Regulars, and newly added short-term Florida militia volunteers would apply the necessary pressure through coercion on the Seminoles' linchpin of their hamlets and force them to end the violence and abide by the accelerated treaty stipulations. Thus, General Clinch would have ended the Second Seminole War before it began, or so he desired and planned. The Seminoles had other plans in mind, plans that they had been refining, coordinating, and patiently waiting to execute for nearly a year.

As an officer in the United States Army and a graduate of the military academy at West Point, Captain Belton did not truly have much of a choice professionally not to obey his superior's lawful order. Captain Belton noted his own concerns with the order he received on 16 December 1835 ordering him to strip his post of the Regulars and send them through enemy territory to reinforce the commander's expedition. Balancing the immediate responsibility to the defense of his post as acting commandant of the fort with the responsibility and loyalty to his commanding officer, General Clinch, Captain Belton delayed. Captain Belton was faced with a "not if but when" question to dispatch Captain Gardiner and Captain Fraser's companies on the road to Fort King. Knowing the dangers and the growing violence of the Seminoles, holding the security of the fort as preeminent, feeling the pressure as each day passed after 16 December, not knowing the security situation at Fort King, Captain Belton delayed for as long as he reasoned was ethically allowed. Reinforcements came from Key West, not the other two companies of which Captain Belton wanted but a portion, a detachment under Major Dade.

Captain Belton had wanted to send all four companies to General Clinch at once. Major Dade's detachment's arrival from Key West was the trigger point and with a filled-out roster of two companies, Captain Belton ordered the detachment to march in compliance with the orders of General Clinch on 23 December 1835. Captain Belton intimately faced one of the costs of command. In the end, it was his decision, watching those sky blue-clad Soldiers marching out the gates of Fort Brooke, which directly affected the lives of his Soldiers.

Vignette: A letter from Lieutenant George McCall describing Fort Brooke soon after its founding in 1824:

"My dear Father: We have now been established here, I may say, about a month. We are encamped on a point of elevated land lying between the mouth of Hillsborough River and the bay of that name—near its head. Our camp extends under a canopy of the most superb trees I ever beheld; and as the temperature is from 75° to 80° Fahrenheit, you may readily conceive how delightful is the noontide shade they afford. These giant live-oaks throw out their huge limbs at a distance of six to ten feet from the ground; these enormous limbs, as large as the trunks of common trees, extend in an almost horizontal direction for ten or fifteen feet, then spreading and rising to the height of fifty or sixty feet, form a dense round head that is a perfect parasol. Their great limbs and their smaller branches are hung with long pendants of the Spanish moss, and with festoons of the yellow jasmine which has been in bloom, with clusters of bright yellow flowers, ever since we have been here. The progress of the work is quite satisfactory. The walls of the men's barracks are already eight or nine feet high; they will be about twelve feet, to give the free circulation of air so essential in a hot climate. These buildings are of pine logs, and are raised by notching the logs down, one upon another. The quarters for the officers will not be commenced until the barracks for the men are roofed in and floored." (McCall, 133).

Analysis:

1. Having heard the threats and knowing of the growing violence and the dangers posed to traveling through the Seminole Nation; did General Clinch make a sound military decision with the information on hand? Why or why not?

2. Were Captain Belton's actions appropriate to delay as long as he thought possible and in the end send two companies as ordered though he personally disagreed with the order?

3. What role, if any, did the US Army leaderships' perception of the Seminoles' influence the decision to send minimal force among a noted larger gathering of potentially hostile enemy? How is this similar to our modern military's perceptions of other cultures and its influence on our military decision making?

Stand Two

Hillsborough River Crossing and Fort Foster

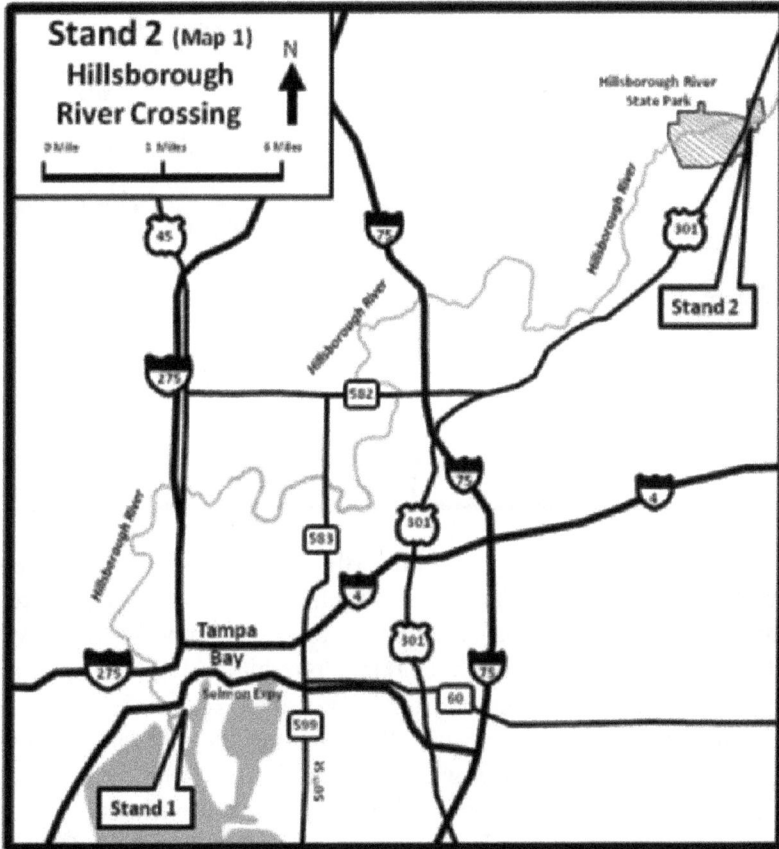

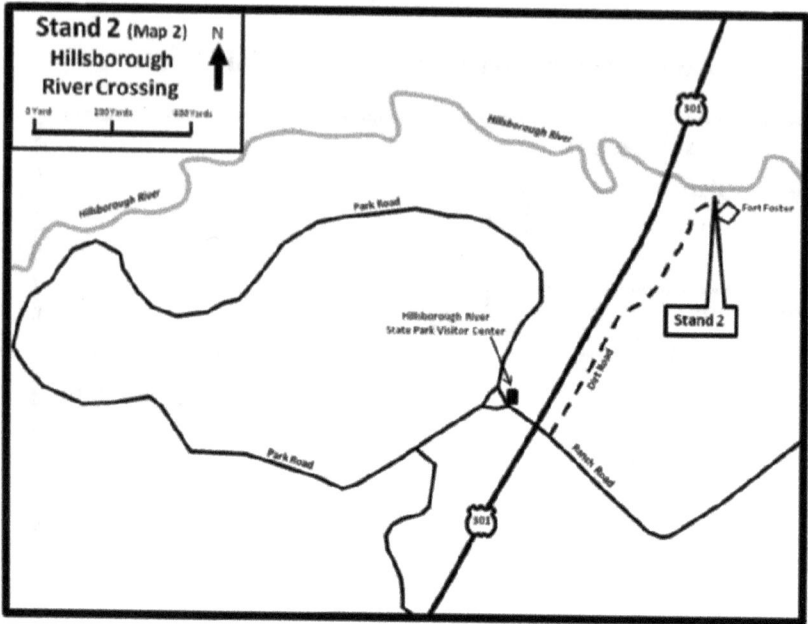

Stand 2 (Map 2)
Hillsborough
River Crossing

Directions: From Stand One, travel north on Old Water Street toward Channelside Drive (.1 miles) and turn slightly left on East Brorein Street (.1 miles). Continue veering slightly left to enter Selmon Expressway Toll East ramp towards Brandon. Continue on Selmon Expressway/State Route-618-TOLL-E (portions toll) for 3.2 miles to Exit 11 US-41 North. Then turn left on South 50th Street/US-41/State Route-599 for 1.2 miles. Merge onto Interstate-4 East toward Orlando for 2.6 miles. Take Exit 7 towards US-301 North/ Zephyrhills/ US-92 East/ Vandenberg Airport for .9 miles then merge onto US-301 North towards Zephyrhills for 14.3 miles. The Hillsborough River State Park Visitor Center will be on the left of US-301. The address is 15402 North US Highway 301. The visitor center is on the left (west) of Highway 301 but the actual stand site is to the right (east) of the highway. Make sure to coordinate with the staff at the visitor center prior to your staff ride to be able to go to the stand site. On the day of the ride, you will need to make a right off Highway 301 on Ranch Road and after only about 40 yards, make a left on to a dirt road. Follow the road to the end where it stops at Fort Foster (a reconstructed fort). The original fort was not built until after the Dade Campaign, thus the stand should focus on the river crossing just north of the fort. Although the fort is not part of this campaign, you can arrange for a tour with the park rangers if time permits.

Visual Aid: Historical Map 2: Area of Dade's March.

Orientation: The Hillsborough River is to the north, one of the major waterways forded by the march since the bridges had been destroyed. Fort Foster was constructed later in the Second Seminole War but marks an important crossing point on the Fort King Road. This was part of the Seminole Nation at the start of the war. In the winter months of the 1830s, the Hillsborough River depth was waist deep. The riverbank heights were gently sloping. Even so, to get the wagon and the gun across the ford due to the burned bridge required a system of ropes and pulleys with brute manpower hauling the equipment across the water and up the banks. (Laumer, 98-99).

Description: One of Major Dade's security measures before he undertook the march to Fort King was the addition of a six-pound artillery piece to the two companies of Soldiers. A few years prior, Major Dade had chosen speed for security when he had made a similar march along a similar route to reinforce the forces to the north of Fort Brooke during a flare up of hostility. His command had made it safely without contest. This time he assessed a different situation and demand a cannon accompany his command, choosing firepower over speed as security for this march to Fort King.

The command was no more than a few hours from Fort Brooke when the cannon's draft team of oxen stopped cold and refused to go on. Highlighting the importance Major Dade placed on the cannon, he only went a few hours march farther from the cannon to the river crossing and stopped, sending an imploring letter back via courier to Captain Belton at Fort Brooke asking for a new team of draft animals be bought to help bring the cannon back to the column. Belton would come through for Dade, his own concerns for the security of the column inspiring him to get the necessary animals and supplies together, resulting in the cannon's return to the Dade's command that night.

On Christmas of 1835, Dade's command neared the crossing of Hillsborough River. The bridges had been burned and were only partially intact. There was not enough of the bridge left to get the wagon and the cannon across. They would have to ford the river. This was the moment the Soldiers thought most vulnerable, their forces split, some on one side, some crossing, and others waiting on the south bank. The cannon, wagon, and caisson had to be manually hauled across the cool river in winter and with ropes pulled up the bank on the other side back to the road. It was back-breaking work, literally, for one Private Thompson who injured his back would be sent back to Fort Brooke on foot alone after Dr. Gatlin determined there was nothing to do for him and he would be of no use in a fight in such pain. The burned bridge was a sure sign of Seminole activity and it, along with the draft animals for the addition of the cannon, added to the delays and cost the Army command time.

Vignette: None

Analysis:

1. Was Major Dade's decision sound to rely on firepower over speed for security and thus bring an artillery piece along though it significantly delayed his movements most notably at the fording of the Withlachoochie? These are perennial considerations for any movement conducted through enemy territory, speed or firepower.

2. Was the US Army correct in determining the river crossings along the Fort King Road were the most dangerous points on the march? If not, why would the Soldiers have come to such a conclusion? If so, were the Seminoles mistaken in not attacking until after the river crossings?

3. How are the route limitations that Major Dade incurred through bringing along a wagon and cannon similar to those faced by the US Army in modern conflicts with irregular opponents in difficult terrain?

Stand Three

Fort King Road

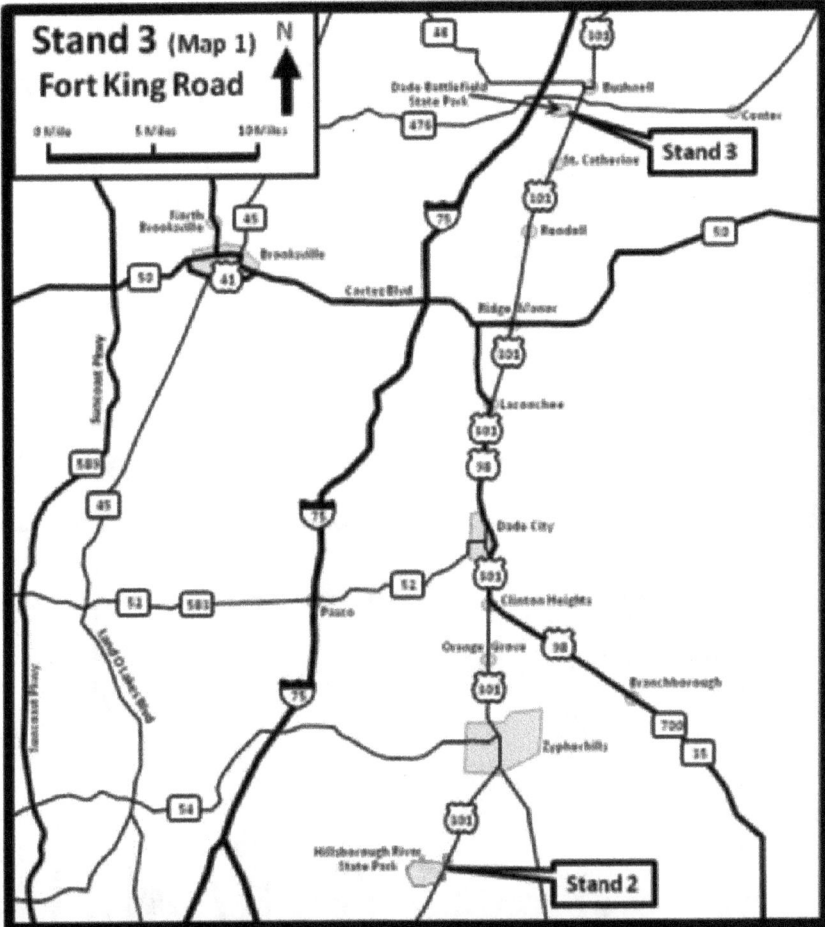

Stand 3 (Map 2)
Fort King Road
N
0 Yard   200 Yards   400 Yards

Stand 3 (Map 3)
Fort King Road
N
0 Yard   50 Yards   100 Yards

Directions: To Stand Three from Stand Two, start north on US-301 for 37 miles. Turn left on Seminole Avenue/CR 476 West, signs for Dade Battlefield Historic State Park will begin. Take a left on Battlefield Drive and continue until it turns into County Road 603. Address for the park is 7200 County Road 603, Bushnell, FL 33513.

From Tampa directly to Stand Three, take 1-75 North towards Ocala for 40 miles. Take Exit 314 State Route-48, towards Bushnell. Keep right to take ramp towards Bushnell and slight right onto State Route-48. You will make a right onto Battlefield Drive/County Road-603 and continue to the park entrance approximately one mile.

Visual Aid: Historical Map 2: Area of Dade's March.

Orientation: The first parking lot to the right is for large vehicles and another additional parking lot is next to the Visitor's Center for smaller vehicles. Stand Three is just south of the recreated breastworks and the Visitor's Center on the small path, which is the remains of the original Fort King Road. It is approximately 15 meters east of the paved trail in front of the Visitor's Center. It is recommended to go to the Visitor's Center after the staff ride to look at exhibits there. The main path through the park is the remains of the original Fort King Road. The road from Fort Brooke to Fort King was 125 miles long, built in early 1828. It was cut through the forest and swamps by a combination of Soldier manual labor as well as that of local Florida settlers' slave labor. For most of the route, the underbrush came right up to the edges of the road and continually encroached on the road. With the road wide enough for one wagon or two mounted horses, about 20 feet, the Soldiers marched in columns of two. The ground was not even as the road had been cut through thick vegetation leaving many stumps and holes. The path itself was extremely sandy causing struggles for wagons and especially heavy items such as cannon and caisson. It has smoothed over with time and is more packed compared to the historical road. In addition, the surrounding grounds are more cleared out and open than before. A look to the natural preservation area to the east of the park/ road will reveal more of the natural terrain closer to what it would have been like at the time of the battle. Towards the northern end of the park and road are white pillars scattered along the road. These are markers erected in remembrance of the fallen officers of the advance party and the initial attack. They are approximately where the bodies fell.

Description: The road expedited movement through the thick vegetation that surrounded the area. With the wagon supplies and the cannon and caisson, the Soldiers had no choice but to take this one road through the

Seminole Nation. The road connected the two primary US Army posts in north-central Florida and was well traveled by companies moving back and forth and courier travel in times of peace. During the march itself, the command was broken up into three distinct groups as they moved along the Fort King Road.

There was an advance guard made up of a squad of Soldiers, eight Soldiers on day of battle, marching in columns and this was generally led by two officers, a lieutenant and one of the captains. Normally, Major Dade also accompanied the advance guard on his horse along with the translator as he did on the morning of the attack. Also on the day of the fight, Captain Fraser was with the advance guard.

The second element was the main body and this was composed of the majority of the command to include the cannon and supply wagon and medical officer. The other captain and most of the remaining officers marched in columns here. On the day of the attack, Captain Gardiner was with the main body.

The final element was the rear guard. It was led by a lieutenant. The entire column was also supported by flankers, small groups of Soldiers sent out to the sides of the main body. However, these were pulled in once the terrain started to open up the day of the ambush. The entire column at times spanned over 300 meters with the advance guard at times over 200 meters in front of the main body.

Vignette: None

Analysis: There is no specific analysis for the Fort King Road but it may be worth mentioning the terrain and maneuverability aspects relevant to the road's role in the fight. If conducting the seven-stand option, this is the first stand and should include the Decision to March as found in Stand One above.

Stand Four

Seminole Decision to Attack

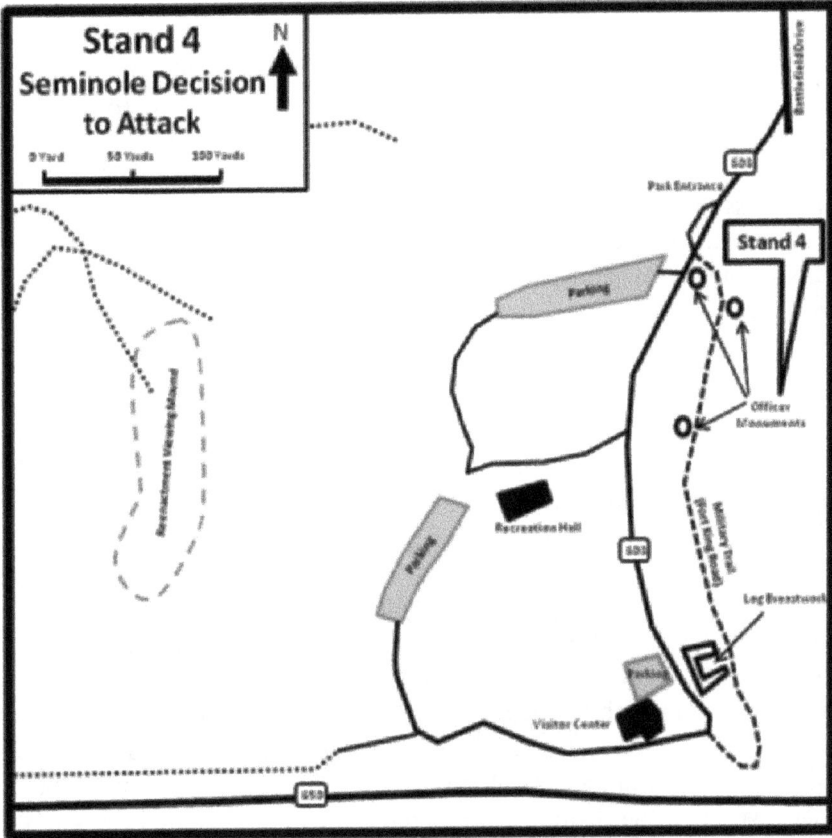

Directions: From Stand Three, walk north along the Fort King Road approximately 200 yards and then turn east and walk off the path another 30 yards until you reach the wire fence of the park's border.

Visual Aid: Historical Map 3: Initial Assault.

Orientation: Facing west is the road on which the US Army Soldiers marched north, behind the stand to the east, was the large pond. To the east and south were the swampland and more dense growth with scattered ponds. Further south were the previously forded rivers. North about 40 miles was Fort King, the Soldiers' destination. This stand is not on the site of the Seminole camp where they made the decision to attack; rather this stand is on the general location of the Seminole battle lines. The decision to attack was made the night before the battle, several miles south of this location.

Description: Having received the culturally required higher Seminole Nation leadership in the form of Micanopy, the Seminoles were ready to execute their ambush on the night of the 27 December, 1835. A portion of the Seminole forces had been trailing the marching Soldiers since they departed Fort Brooke on 23 December. The Seminoles had wished to strike at the Soldiers three days earlier and deeper into the tangled dense underbrush near one of the more dangerous crossing points over a river but they had needed a senior chief's presence. With the arrival of Chief Micanopy, they decided they did not need to wait for Osceola's presence as he was already involved in his strike against Agent Thompson at Fort King. Still, Micanopy hesitated and preached caution and inaction. The junior chiefs, Alligator and Jumper, upbraided him and challenged him to action. He characteristically succumbed to their manipulation and pressure.

They chose an open dry portion of the Fort King Road just beyond the final river crossing for Major Dade's column and just before the end of the swampland. The Seminoles, afraid that the chance would pass the closer the Soldiers came to Fort King and further from the swamp, chose land that benefited the maneuverability of the mounted Seminole force and gave the ambushed Soldiers limited cover to break contact. The presence of underbrush played to Seminole concealment for the ambush. The limited scattered pines gave the Seminoles the degree of cover they needed from the solitary cannon and musket fire of the Soldiers. They initiated the ambush at such a place as to pin one flank of the Soldiers against a large body of water in a pond, block further forward progress with an unengaged mounted force, leaving the Soldiers but two areas to maneuver, into the Seminole dismounted fire or retrograde back into the dense swampland. This same swampland on the edge of the engagement also provided the Seminoles with a sanctuary to retreat.

Ambushes and raids are not purely the purview of the small guerilla-band type of soldiery. However, by necessity, they excel at it or else they would not survive against a stronger force.

Vignette: In the single Seminole record of the attack, one of the main chiefs recounts their decision making:

> Here we thought it best to assail them and should we be defeated, the Swamp would be safe place of retreat. Our scouts were out from the time the Soldiers left the post and reported each night their place of encampment. It was our intention to attack them on the third night but the absence of Oseola [sic] and Micanopy presented

it. On the arrival of the latter, it was agreed not to wait for Oseola, as the favorable moment would pass. Micanopy was timid and urged delay. Jumper earnestly opposed it and reproached the old chief for his indecision. He addressed the Indians and requested those who had faint hearts to remain behind he was going, when Micanopy said he was ready… we moved out of the swamp into the pine-barren… Upon approaching the road, each man chose his position on the west side; opposite, on the east side, there was a pond. Every warrior was protected by a tree or secreted in the high palmettos. (Account of Alligator as told to Captain John Sprague in Sprague, 90).

Analysis:

1. Was the Seminoles' site selection criteria sound for an ambush? Why or why not?

2. How does the site selection for the actual compare to the potential ambush site at the Hillsborough River crossing?

3. Was this action a risk or a gamble for the Seminoles? In the course of this analysis, get the students to define risk and gamble. You can also discuss the concept of mitigation of risk.

4. What are the modern principles of a successful ambush and did the Seminole ambush meet them?

Stand Five
Ambush and Major Dade's Death

Stand 5
Ambush and Major Dade's Death
N

0 Yard   50 Yards   100 Yards

Battlefield Drive

Stand 5

601

Park Entrance

Parking

Reenactment Viewing Mound

Officer Monuments

Military Trail (Fort King Road)

Recreation Hall

Parking

601

Log Breastwork

Parking

Visitor Centre

685

Directions: From Stand Four, return to the Fort King Road and move north 20 yards. Do the stand here on Fort King Road.

Visual Aid: Historical Map 3: Initial Assault.

Orientation: From here to the south approximately 200 yards was the main body of Soldiers. Beyond that were the wagon and cannon followed by the rear guard. To the north and the west were scattered Seminoles with the large pond to the east. The markers are erected at the historical sites where the advance guard's officers were shot.

Description: The US Army Regulars broke camp at about 0500 hours on 28 December 1835 and began their march northward to Fort King in three groups: an advance party, main party with cannon and wagon, and a rear guard. They marched in columns of twos. Major Dade, Captain Fraser, and Lieutenant Mudge led the advance guard while Lieutenant Bassinger commanded the cannon team with Captain Gardiner in the main body. Dr. Gatlin was on the wagon, and the other lieutenants were scattered among the Soldiers of the main and rear guard.

Each prior day, as they passed through the more dangerous grounds, the likely ambush sites, Major Dade posted flankers/skirmishers, and each night he took the extra precaution to order breastworks thrown up and sentries posted. After they passed the last of these suspected ambush sites at the river crossings and entered more open land, Major Dade recalled his flankers from moving in the underbrush of the open territory. He claimed the eye could see as well as the flankers could in the open lands and that the underbrush would slow the flankers' movement and thus that of the column. With the cool, damp weather, Major Dade allowed his men to button their overcoats around their cartridge boxes and muskets, thus hindering any quick employment of these weapons. Premature announcements of coming celebration and enjoyments at the end of the march potentially distracted the vigilance of the column as they now had their mind's eye on scenes of Christmas celebration and relaxation.

Only four hours march from the Soldiers' last night's camp, the Seminoles lay in wait 30 yards from the edge of the road, unseen by the Soldiers in the tall grass or behind the pine trees. With a war whoop from Jumper and the signal shot from Chief Micanopy, the ambush was initiated. Micanopy's first shot rang out sometime between 0800 and 0900 hours on the morning of 28 December. The Seminoles had waited until the entire US Army column had passed in front of them, between them and the pond. With the signal shot from Micanopy that struck down Major Dade, the entire Seminole line fired the initial deadly volley. The entire advance guard was killed where they were marching, as fire swept down the rest of the command, half of the Soldiers were out of the fight in the first volley fired by Seminoles extremely close to the close-ordered column marching Soldiers. All the officers were struck down, either wounded or killed, except for Captain Gardiner, Lieutenant Bassinger, and Dr. Gatlin. Both Lieutenant Keyes and Lieutenant Henderson would survive the first volley but of the two, only Henderson could continue fighting even with a severely wounded arm.

Vignette: Both of these vignettes – the two leading eyewitness accounts, one from Private Clark and the other from a Seminole chief Alligator – recount the critical opening volley and its destructive aftermath. Clark:

"Suddenly I heard a rifle shot in the direction of the advanced guard and this was immediately followed by a musket shot from that quarter. Captain Fraser had rode by me a moment before in that direction. I never saw him afterwards. I had not time to think of the meaning of these shots, before a volley, as if from a thousand rifles, poured in upon us from the front, and all along our left flank. I looked around me and it seemed as if I was the only one left standing in the right wing. Neither could I, until several vollies [sic] had been fired at us, see an enemy and when I did, I could only see their head and arms peering from the long grass, far and near, and from behind the pine trees. The ground seemed to me an open pine barren, no hammock near that I could see. On our right, and a little to our rear, was a large pond of water some distance off. All around us were heavy pine trees, very open, particularly towards the left, and abounding with long high grass. The first fire of the Indians was the most destructive, seemingly killing or disabling one half our men." (Account of Private Ransom Clark as reproduced in Laumer, 236)

Alligator:

About nine o'clock in the morning the command approached. In advance some distance was an officer on a horse, who, Micanopy said, was the captain [Major Dade]; he knew him personally; had been his friend at Tampa. So soon *all* the Soldiers were opposite between us and the pond, perhaps 20 yards off, Jumper gave the whoop, Micanopy fired the first rifle, the signal agreed upon, when every Indian arose and fired, which laid upon the ground, dead, more than half the white men. (Account of Alligator as told to Cpt. John Sprague in Sprague, 90-91)

Analysis:

1. Historically, one of the most damning post facto judgments has been on Major Dade's security the morning of the attack. Are these attacks justified? Could things have been different if flankers were employed or if the Soldiers had kept their muskets at the ready even in the damp conditions?

2. Could any options available to Major Dade at the time have averted this defeat or was the Seminole plan too much to overcome?

3. What were the effects, if any, were there to the loss of leadership for the US Army Regulars?

4. What were the effects, for both Seminoles and US Soldiers, of the first Seminole volley?

Stand Six

Soldiers Rally and Seminoles Retreat

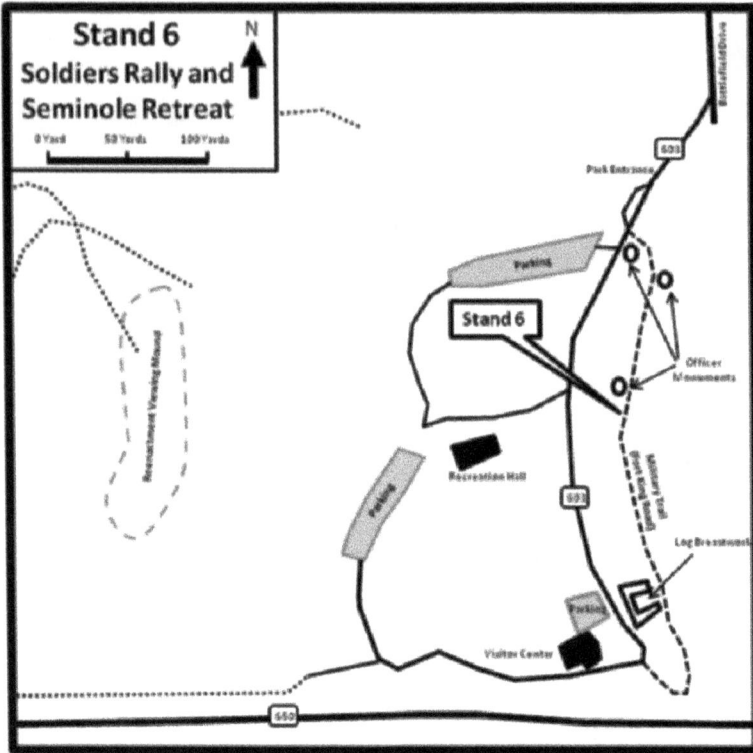

Stand 6
Soldiers Rally and Seminole Retreat

0 Yard   50 Yards   100 Yards

N

Battlefield Drive

Park Entrance

Parking

Stand 6

Officer
Monuments

Recruitment Viewing Mound

Recreation Hall

Parking

Military Trail
(Fort King Road)

Log Breastwork

Parking

Visitor Center

Directions: From Stand Five, move south approximately 100 yards remaining on Fort King Road to arrive at Stand Six.

Visual Aids: Historical Map 3: Initial Assault, Historical Map 4: Final Assault.

Orientation: To the north lies the fallen advance guard where they stood and to the south was the rear guard, wagon, and cannon. The Seminoles were all along the west and across the north with the pond closing off the east.

Description: The initial response to the ambush was surprise and chaos but quickly the Soldiers began to return fire and scatter to the trees to fight in "woodland drill." The Seminoles were well concealed but their fire was less effective after the initial volley and speedily the artillerymen brought the lone six-pounder into action. The most exposed group of Soldiers were those manning the cannon and they suffered from concentrated Seminole fire each time the smoke from the cannon fire cleared. The artillerymen who fell were immediately replaced in order to keep the cannon, under the command of Lieutenant Bassinger, in operation. The cannon was unlimbered and when placed into the action, fired, sweeping from west to north to west from its place in the middle of the road.

The few remaining officers, notably Captain Gardiner and Lieutenant Bassinger, who survived the first volley, rallied the troops exhorting them and leading by example. The Soldiers kept up an increased musketry fire and though the cannon fired high over the heads of the Seminoles, it kept up a rapid fire, adding to the din and active US Army response to the ambush.

The heavy firing of the initial assault lasted from the opening shot between 0800 hours and 0900 hours until around 1400 hours when the Seminoles broke contact and moved northwest just under a mile away to reconsolidate and regroup. The Soldiers had survived the first assault but at terrific loss in both Soldiers and leadership.

Vignette: Seminole chief Alligator described the battle's initial action and the determined leadership and rally of the US Army:

"…when every Indian arose and fired, which laid upon the ground, dead, more than half the white men. The cannon was discharged several times but the men who loaded it were shot down as soon as the smoke cleared away… The Soldiers shouted and whooped and the officers shook their swords and swore. There was a little man, a great brave, who shook his sword at the Soldiers and said, 'God-dam!' no rifle-ball could hit him. As we were returning to the swamp, supposing all were dead an Indian came up and said the white men were building a fort of logs." (Account of Alligator as told to Cpt. John Sprague in Sprague, 91)

Analysis:

1. What factors accounted for the Soldiers' rally after the devastating initial volley?

2. Why did he Seminoles' retreat? Was it the cannon, the musketry of the scattered "Light Infantry" fighting, or something else?

3. What role, if any, did the remaining officers play in the rally?

4. What can be learned by junior leaders today from the initial reaction of the surviving US Army leaders of Dade's fight?

Stand Seven

The Breastworks and Last Stand

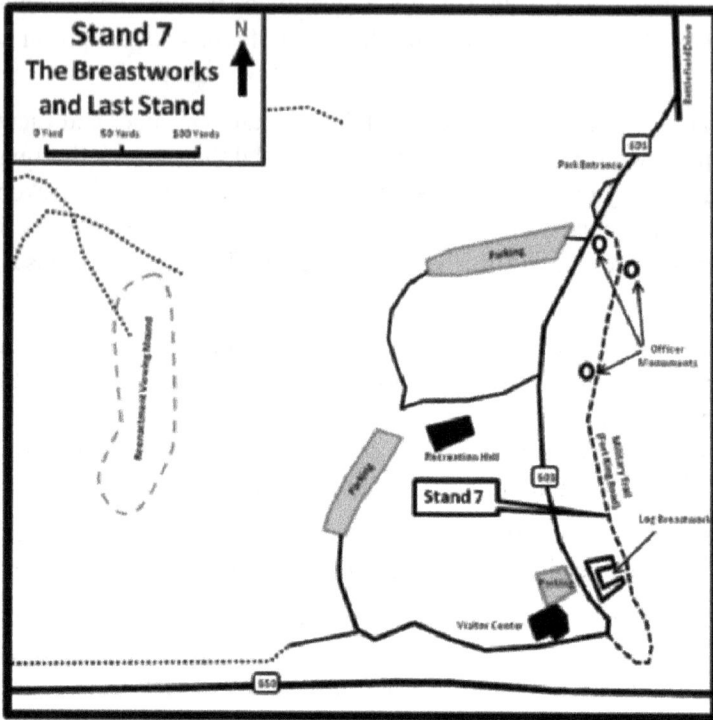

Directions: From Stand Six, proceed south 35 yards just north of the recreated breastworks for Stand Seven, still on the Fort King Road.

Visual Aid: Historical Map 4: Final Assault.

Orientation: Immediately southwest is the location where the breastworks were constructed. The northeast corner of the works was anchored by the cannon while the Seminoles were re-grouping, just under a mile to the northeast. The Seminoles returned while the breastworks were being constructed and they enveloped the Soldiers from the north, west, and south and cornered them in the breastworks.

Description: The command originally had been Captain Gardiner's before the march and then devolved to Major Dade for personal reasons and then returned to Captain Gardiner when Dade was killed in the opening salvo of the ambush. Thus Captain Gardiner made the final decisions affecting the Soldiers on that day. With half the US Army force out of the fight in the first volley and the engagement of the cannon the only thing to deny the

Seminoles complete victory in the first assault, Captain Gardiner made his decision to stay and fight, basing his defense around the cannon, gathering the wounded and throwing up impromptu breastworks.

This decision in effect determined the fate of the Soldiers. Captain Gardiner decided to leave no man behind. The wounded could not be left to the hands of the Seminoles and Fort Brooke and Fort King were far away for the transport of so many wounded by so few able-bodied survivors. Lastly, he could not utilize the cannon effectively in maneuver. These considerations led Captain Gardiner to make his quick decision to remain and fight until the end, keeping faith with the wounded and staying with the weapon that had kept them alive that long. The US forces were outnumbered. The closest friendly forces could only be reached by forcing through the enemy positions and into even more open land being watched by a horse-mounted enemy force. Retrograde movement returned to the more dense and restricted terrain in swampland, preferred and known by the enemy far better than the Soldiers, and indeed, the more conducive sites for ambush in the minds of the Soldiers.

Captain Gardiner took control and gave the orders. Some Soldiers began felling the young sapling trees to make the breastworks while others gathered the wounded and brought them back to the works and checked the dead and wounded for ammunition.

The Seminoles gathered less than a mile away over a small knoll and when they learned of the entrenching Soldiers, they debated a second assault. It was the exhortations of the two younger chiefs, Jumper and Alligator that shamed the others into finishing the Soldiers off at their breastworks. After less than an hour lull, around 1500 hours, the Seminoles approached the works. They spread out in the face of the booming cannon and the musket fire of the remaining 30 capable defenders. The cannon was placed along the north wall of the breastworks with the same field of fire as before, west to north. The limber and the chest were brought into the breastworks within the perimeter. The Seminoles enveloped the position, forcing those Soldiers who were fighting behind trees outside the fortification to move to it and trapping the remaining Soldiers. In time the rifle fire took its toll and the Soldiers expended the last of their ammunition and the Seminoles pressed in against the reduced resistance.

Vignette: Private Clark's account of the Dade's command's last stand is poignant in its subtle description of the Soldiers' desperation and determination. By this time the Soldiers knew all was lost but still fought on as the Seminoles advanced again. In the surviving soldier's words:

> We had barely raised our breastworks knee high when we again saw the Indians advancing in great numbers over the hill to our left. They came on boldly till within a long musket shot when they spread themselves from tree to tree to surround us. We immediately extended as Light Infantry, covering ourselves by the trees, and opening a brisk fire from cannon and musketry. The former I don't think could have done much mischief, the Indians were so scattered... Lieutenant Henderson had his left arm broken but he continued to load his musket and to fire it, resting on the stump, until he was finally shot down towards the close of the second attack, and during the day he kept up his spirits and cheered the men. Lieutenant Keyes had both his arms broken in the first attack; they were bound up and slung in a handkerchief and he sat for the remainder of the day until he was killed- reclining against the breastwork- his head often reposing upon it- regardless of everything that was passing around him. Our men were by degrees all cut down. We had maintained a steady fire from 8 until 2 P.M. or thereabout... had been pretty busily engaged for more than five hours. Lieutenant B [Bassinger] was the only officer left alive and he severely wounded. He told me as Indians approached, to lay down and feign myself dead. I looked through the logs and saw the savages approaching in great numbers. (Account of Private Ransom Clark as reproduced in Laumer, 237-238)

Analysis:

1. Critique Captain Gardiner's decision to build the breastworks and remain in place. What were his other options? Was he correct to remain?

2. What caused the culminating defeat, was it Seminole superiority in numbers, the Soldiers' expenditure of ammunition, or something else?

3. How do the final defensive principles exhibited by Dade's men compare to those used in modern missions?

Stand Eight

Death of Captain Gardiner and the Fate of the Survivors

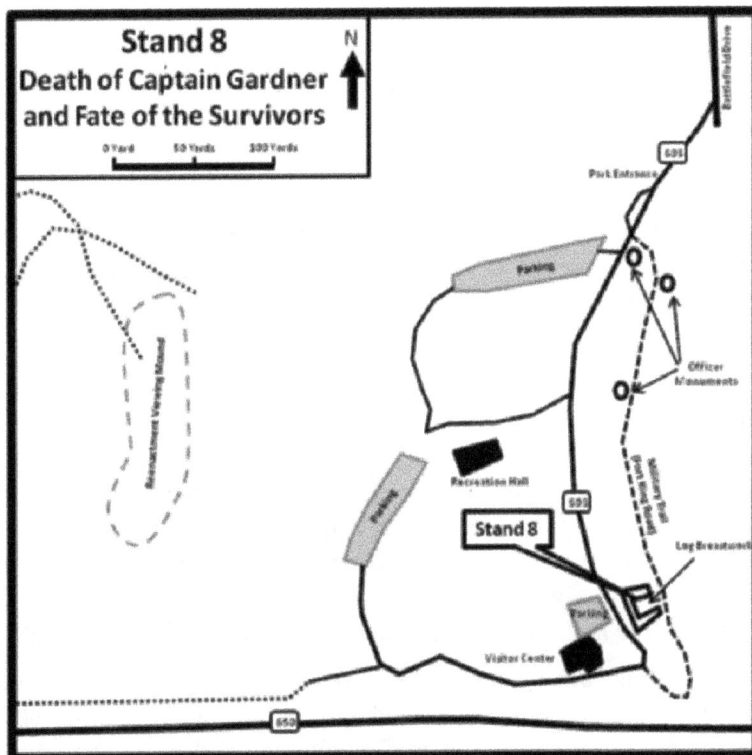

Directions: From Stand Seven, move approximately 10 yards to the southwest at the nearest corner of the recreated Breastworks for Stand Eight.

Visual Aid: Historical Map 4: Final Assault.

Orientation: The remaining Soldiers were contained within the breastworks or immediately outside it manning the cannon. They were arrayed along the north, east, and south portions of the triangle to confront the Seminoles. None faced the east, the pond, and no Seminoles attacked from that direction.

Description: Captain Gardiner fell in the center of the works, mortally wounded, passing command to the one remaining officer, Lieutenant Bassinger. The Seminoles kept up their rifle fire until there remained no more resistance. Bassinger commanded those left to play dead. The Soldiers had expended all their ammunition, the cannon had its final 50th round loaded but no one was left to fire it having all been wounded or confined to the works by the encroaching Seminoles tightening the noose. It was nearing late afternoon when the firing ceased.

Without resistance, the Seminoles approached the breastworks. First, Chief Micanopy gave a speech, gesturing to the works. No doubt he praised the Seminole victory over the perceived superiority of the "white man" and his professional army. The Seminoles were so confident in their victory that they entered the works without guard and ignored those wounded, taking what military equipment and supplies they could as well as weapons and the culturally obligatory scalps. Some US Army wounded gave struggle and struck at the Seminoles only to be killed themselves as they tried to escape the triangle wooden enclosure.

With their military victory over Major Dade's command complete, the Seminoles took their military plunder and their scalps of the dead and moved north, towards Osceola and the Seminoles gathering from Fort King to celebrate their dual victories over Major Dade's command and the murder of Indian Affairs Agent Thompson. As they left the enclosure and the wounded, the African-Americans who had accompanied the Seminoles came to the breastworks. These Africans were mounted and numbered around fifty and had refrained from the fighting, most likely because they had been part of the mounted blocking force to the north of the fighting.

These Seminole allies entered the wooden enclosure and took to executing the wounded Soldiers. After they executed all those who they noticed were still alive and took what few clothing and belongings they desired, though not much, they too followed the route of the departing Seminoles, killing the draft animals, lighting the wagon on fire and tossing the cannon into the nearby pond.

After they had left some of the few remaining Soldiers stirred from their false deaths. One would be shot attempting to run from the enclosure, motivating the others to wait until dark. The only other two who remained left together around 2100 hours, heading back south towards Fort Brooke and away from the direction the Seminoles had taken, even though Fort King was much closer. They moved south only to run into a mounted Seminole the following day. They split up, the Seminole rode down and killed one survivor, but Private Clark eluded capture and crawled, dragged, himself back to Fort Brooke over two days later. The only other survivor of the fight to return to Fort Brooke did so earlier but he had left wounded before the last stand, Private Joseph Sprague.

Vignette: Private Ransom Clark's account of the battle imparts the excitement and terror involved in close quarters combat and survival of the defeated. He wrote of the enemy occupation of the Soldiers' defenses and resulting actions of the belligerents:

A heavy made Indian, of middle stature, painted down to the waist, [Micanopy] seemed to be the Chief. He made them a speech, frequently pointing to the breastwork. At length they charged into the work; there was none to offer resistance, and they did not seem to suspect the wounded being alive- offering no indignity, but stepping about carefully quietly stripping off our accoutrements, and carrying away our arms. They then retired in a body in the direction from whence they came. Immediately upon their retreat, fort or fifty negroes on horseback galloped up... and commenced with horrid shouts and yells the butchery of the wounded... Lieutenant B [Bassinger] hearing the negroes butchering the wounded at length sprang up, and asked them to spare his life. They met him with the blows of their axes, and their fiendish laughter. Having been wounded in five different places myself, I was pretty well covered with blood, and two scratches that I had received on my head, gave to me the appearance of having been shot through the brain... After stripping all the dead in this manner, they trundled off the cannon in the direction the Indians had gone, and went away... Shortly after the negroes went away, one Wilson... crept from under some of the dead bodies... He asked me to go with him back to the Fort, and I was going to follow him, when, as he jumped over the breastwork, an Indian sprang from behind a tree and shot him down. I then lay quiet until 9 o'clock that night, when D. Cony, the only living soul beside myself; and I started, upon our journey. We knew it was nearest to go to Fort King, but we did not know the way, and we had seen the enemies retreat in that direction. As I came out, I saw Dr. G. [Gatlin] lying stripped amongst the dead. The last I saw of him whilest living, was kneeling behind the breast-work, with two double barrel guns by him, and he said, 'Well, I have got four barrels for them!' Captain G. [Gardiner] after being severely wounded, cried out, 'I can give you no more orders, my lads, do your best!' I last saw a negro spurn his body, saying with an oath, 'that's one of their officers-'... My comrade and myself got along quite well until the next day, when we met an Indian on horseback... coming up the road. I took the right, and he the left of the road. The Indian pursued him. Shortly afterwards I heard a rifle shot and a little after another... I made something of a circuit before I struck the beaten track again. That night I was a good deal annoyed by the wolves, who had scented my blood, and came very close to me; the next day, the 30th, I reached the Fort. (Account of Private Ransom Clark as reproduced in Laumer, 239)

Analysis:

1. Why did the Seminoles act with restraint once they had taken the breastworks in contrast to the actions of the accompanying African-Americans?

2. When faced with an alien culture (Seminoles, their slaves, or Al Qaeda for example in this day), what needs to be done to understand that culture and maintain discipline even if faced with enemies who employ techniques that we do not condone?

Stand Nine

The Aftermath

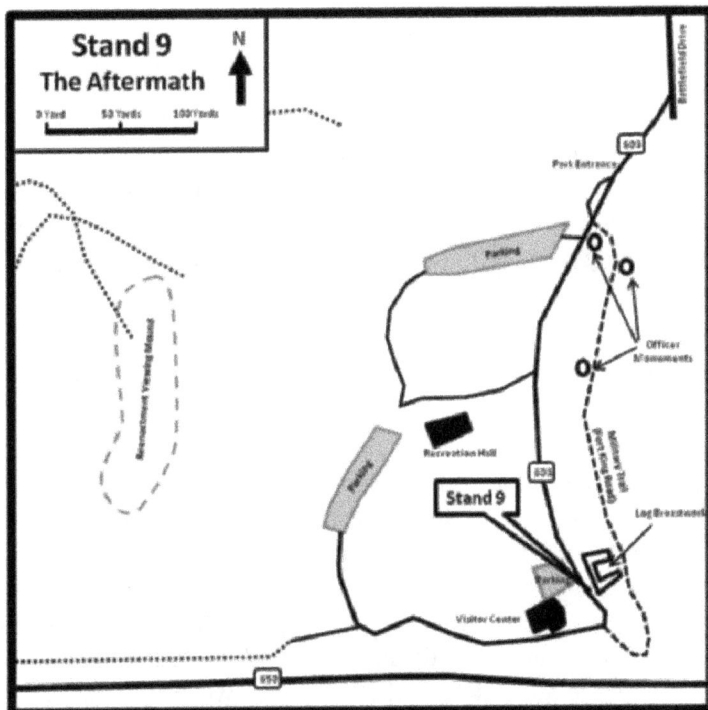

Directions: Move southwest from the recreated Breastworks less than five yards to the paved trail in front of the Visitor's Center to arrive at Stand Nine, the final stop.

Visual Aid: Historical Map 4: Final Assault.

Orientation: The Visitor's Center is to the west, the parking lots to the northwest. Directly to the east are the breastworks, to the south along Fort King Road is the route the US Army survivors took after darkness fell back towards Fort Brooke.

Description: The site of Dade's Battle would remain untouched after the last African allied with the Seminoles departed north toward Fort King and the two wounded Soldiers headed south to Fort Brooke. It was a larger contingent of Regulars and Louisiana volunteers under Brigadier General Gaines from New Orleans that first traced Major Dade's route along the Fort King Road in response to the report of Private Clark. They would not arrive at the site of the battle until nearly two months later, in February

1836. Since then the Second Seminole War was in full swing. In fact, one of the largest battles of the war was fought only a few days following Dade's Battle by Brigadier General Clinch, ignorant of the fate of Major Dade's contingent but impatiently having undertaken his campaign against the Seminole hamlets north of the Withlacoochie.

The columns under General Gaines came across the site of Dade's last stand and after proper identification and accountability, interred the remains of the fallen Soldiers. Playing the Death March with friends of the officers and the regimental band of Major Dade's own regiment, the 4th Infantry, leading the way, circled the hasty memorial and burial grounds before continuing on to war and more battles with the Seminole Nation.

The United States Army went on to a frustrating Second Seminole War where thousands of volunteers flocked to avenge this "massacre" and many Florida militia came to defend their right to expansion while more and more Regulars cycled through service in hot, humid, frustrating Florida. The Army struggled to find the enemy and in time shifted course to targeting homesteads and livelihoods, persuading the shadowy Seminoles that living in fear was worse than living west of the Mississippi. The war officially ended on 14 August 1842 as declared by Colonel William Worth, the last in a long line of Army commanders sent to quell the Seminoles. By this time, after nearly seven years of fighting, the US military through military, and political methods had whittled the remaining stubborn Seminoles down to about six hundred. Colonel Worth said the remaining could be removed "by pacific and persuasive measure, or not at all." Even with half the entire regular Army the US could not cover the entire 47,000 square miles of Florida to hunt down the less than one thousand Seminoles remaining.

By the end of 1843, 3,824 Seminoles had been successfully shipped west out of Florida. The US Army Regulars suffered 1,466 dead, of which only 328 were killed in battle. The militia numbers and those of the volunteers are unrecorded. In 1836 alone, 17 percent of the commissioned officers in the US Army resigned their commissions due in large part to the escalating war in Florida. Dade's Battle Was the beginning of a long and bloody war.

Vignette: Acting Inspector General Captain Ethan Allen Hitchcock's report upon reaching the site of Dade's Battle would be a significant document in both the historical recreation of the event as well as the contemporary "call to arms" for more troops to fight the growing war. He wrote:

General- Agreeably to your directions, I observed the battle ground six or seven mile north of the Withlacoochee River, where Major Dade and his command were destroyed by the Seminole Indians... and have the honor to submit the following report... Our advance guard had passed the ground without halting, when the General and his Staff came upon one of the most appalling scenes that can be imagined. We first saw some broken and scattered bones; then a cart, the oxen of which were lying dead... a little to the right, one of two horses were seen. We then came to a small enclosure, made by felling trees in such a manner as to form a triangular breast-work for defense. Within the triangle, along the north and west faces of it, were about thirty bodies, mostly mere skeletons, although much of the clothing was left upon them. These were lying, ever one of them, in precisely the same position they must have occupied during the fight; their heads next to the logs over which they had delivered their fire, and their bodies stretched with striking regularity parallel to each other. They had evidently been shot dead at their posts, and the Indians had not disturbed them, except by taking the scalps of most of them. Passing this little breast-work, we found other bodies along the road, and by the side of the road, generally behind tees, which had been resorted to for cover from there enemies' fire. Advancing about two hundred yards farther, we found a cluster of bodies in the middle of the road. They were evidently the advanced guard, in the lead of which was the body of Major Dade, and to the right that of Captain Fraser... we had with us many of the personal friends of the officers of Major Dade's command, and it is gratifying to be able to state, that every officer as identified by undoubted evidence. They were buried, and the cannon... that the Indians had thrown into a swamp, was recovered and placed vertically at the head of the grave, where it is to be hoped it will long remain. The bodies of the non-commissioned officers and the privates were buried in two graves, and it was ground that ever man was accounted for. (Report of Captain Hitchcock, dated February 22, 1836 as reproduced in Cohen, 74-75)

Analysis:

1. Historians with hindsight claim Dade's Battle was merely a Seminole "tactical" victory and never had the potential to be anything more? If this is a legitimate assessment, how is it so? If not, why?

2. How do the Seminole actions, tactics, plans, motivations reflect insurgencies the United States Army has fought in its history, or insurgency warfare in general?

Part IV. Integration
Final Phase of the Staff Ride

As this handbook has previously emphasized, a staff ride consists of three phases. The first phase is the "Preliminary Study Phase." This phase is conducted before the visit to the battlefield and prepares the students for the visit. The second phase is the "Field Study Phase." This phase is conducted on the battlefield and enables students to understand historical events through analysis of the actual terrain. The final phase of a staff ride is the "Integration Phase." No staff ride is complete without an integration phase because it is critical for the students to understand what happened, why it happened, and most importantly, what can be learned from the study of the battle or campaign.

There are several factors that the staff ride leader should consider when planning for and conducting the integration phase. First, the leader must work with the organization that is participating in the ride and select a time and location for the integration session. Occasionally, units may have to depart shortly after the last stand of the field phase and the staff ride leader must conduct the integration phase on the battlefield immediately after completing the field study phase. However, when possible, students should have some time for personal reflection and thought before the integration phase. Thus, the integration phase is best if conducted the day after the field study phase ends. Even if you cannot wait an extra day, it is best to do the integration session at a location different from the last stand, a place comfortable and dry that will encourage open discussion from all the participants.

The staff ride leader should organize the integration phase based on the unit as well as time available and training objectives. The leader can conduct the integration phase in any format or may simply lead a discussion with participants on what they learned. Specific students can brief particular items or just have an open discussion with minimal structure. It is important to keep in mind that the integration phase is not an AAR (after action review) of the ride itself, i.e., ways to improve the ride. While it is useful to seek constructive criticism in order to continue to improve the ride, this should be done at another time or perhaps with written AAR comments. Instead, the integration phase is used for the students of the campaign to integrate their preliminary study with the fieldwork in order to gain insights that are relevant to their current duties and enhance their professional development. Whatever method the staff ride leader chooses to employ, the most important thing to remember is that the participants should do the majority of the talking.

One method that often produces a fruitful integration phase is to conduct the session in three parts based on three broad questions. Sometimes the leader need only present one of these general questions and let others carry the conversation or the leader may have to ask more follow-up questions to prod the discussion. Each of the three questions is discussed below.

What aspects and impressions of the campaign had you developed in the preliminary study phase that changed or were strongly reinforced because of your study of the ground?

This is a crucial question because seeing the terrain is central to a staff ride, otherwise the campaign could simply be studied in the classroom. Of course, students may develop a wide range of answers based on personal study and observations in the field. Some of the more popular aspects of the discussion of terrain for Dade's Battle include Major Dade's assessment on impact on security, the Seminoles' site selection of the ambush, the restriction of the road on maneuver for the Soldiers, the availability of cover and concealment for the initial ambushers and the rallied Soldiers, and Captain Gardiner's decision to make a stand. The staff ride leader can ask a related question which may also generate good discussion: Did seeing the terrain alter your opinion of any of the leaders and their decisions?

What aspects of warfare have changed and what aspects have remained the same since Dade's Battle?

The answers to the "changed" aspects will probably seem more obvious to the modern military professional and often will be related to technology. This may include changes in weapons, communications, and numerous other pieces of equipment. The aspects that have "remained the same" may not seem as numerous at first but the students will often build on some initial answers and find many good items. The role of key personalities, the importance of intelligence, the need for strong positive leadership and an ability to motivate Soldiers, the importance of maneuverability, warrior ethos, elements of surprise, courage, and fear are just some of the items of warfare that seem to have changed little since 1835. Depending on the group, you may want to ask a few more focused questions. For example, if you have an infantry unit, you can ask the following: What aspects of an ambush have changed and what aspects have remained the same?

What insight(s) can the modern military professional gain from Dade's Battle that is relevant today?

Clearly, the participants can take this discussion into a vast number of arenas. Once again, the type of unit participating in the staff ride might help to guide the discussion. For example, a military intelligence unit might focus the commander's situational awareness, intelligence gathering, and the importance of reconnaissance.

These concepts are suggestions. The staff ride leader may use some of them, use another framework, or simply let the students take the discussion in whichever direction they want.

The three suggested integration phase questions are to aid in sparking discussion, not to provide hard and fast "rules" of warfare. Note that the handbook provides examples of possible answers to the questions but it does not attempt to provide a list of "right" answers. The staff ride leader should take time before the session to write down his or her answers to these questions in order to have some potential ideas to generate student discussion. At the same time, the staff ride leader should strive for the participants to develop their own answers and thus be prepared to let the discussion roam many different paths.

Part V. Support
Practical Information on Conducting a Staff Ride in the Tampa and Dade Battlefield Area

1. Information and assistance.

a. The Staff Ride Team, Combat Studies Institute, Fort Leavenworth, Kansas, can provide advice and assistance on every aspect of the staff ride. The Staff Ride Team can also recommend facilitators to lead a Dade's Battle Staff Ride. Visit the Combat Studies Institute website for information on obtaining staff ride assistance and/or leadership. Staff Ride Team support includes background information, knowledge of the battle and battlefield, and familiarity with the Dade's Battle area.

Address: Combat Studies Institute
290 Stimson, Unit 1
Fort Leavenworth, KS 66027
Telephone: DSN: 552-2078
Commercial: (913) 684-2082
Website: http://usacac.army.mil/CAC2/csi/SRTeam.asp

b. The Dade Battle Staff Ride takes place at two Florida Historic State Parks. It is important to contact the staff of both parks and let them know you are conducting a staff ride. Dade Battlefield Historic State Park has a visitor's center on the premises. However, the Fort Foster Historic State Park on the Hillsborough River does not have its own dedicated Visitor's Center as it is part of the larger Hillsborough River State Park and its exhibit is shared in the 1930s Ranger Station.Fort Foster itself is still preserved as a historic site.

Dade Battlefield
Address: 7200 County Road 603
Bushnell, FL, 33513
Telephone: Dade Battlefield Visitor Center
(352) 793 4781
Website: http://www.floridastateparks.org/dadebattlefield/

Fort Foster
Address: 15402 US 301 N.
Thonotasassa, FL 33592
Telephone: Hillsborough River State Park Visitor Center
(813) 987 6771
Website: http://www.floridastateparks.org/fortfoster/

2. Logistics.

a. Meals. There are many restaurants in Tampa that are convenient to hotel locations, and should take care of breakfast and dinner. Lunch can either be a box lunch carried on the vehicles or you can eat at nearby restaurants, although options can be scarce along portions of US 301 between Tampa and Bushnell. Depending on time, there are picnic areas at the primary staff ride location, the Dade Battlefield Historic State Park.

b. Lodging. Groups can find many hotels in the Tampa Bay area if travel time requires they remain over night. If the group wants to cut down on lodging costs, there are many military bases in Florida but most are not as conveniently located as the hotels.

c. Travel. If the group is flying to the area, the Tampa airport is the most convenient to use. Once on the ground, larger groups will need to contract for a bus—make sure it has a microphone and public address system as well as a restroom. Smaller groups (less than 20) might find it easier for parking and maneuvering to use rental vans.

3. Other considerations.

a. A reconnaissance of the stands and route just prior to execution of the ride is imperative for a successful staff ride.

b. Ensure that every member of the group has water. Additionally, Dade Battlefield Historic State Park has public restrooms, however, there are none available at Stand One or Stand Two at Fort Foster which requires additional planning. Make a plan for adequate use of these facilities.

c. Ensure that your group has proper clothing for inclement weather. Thunderstorms can occur in any season. Some walking is required at both the Hillsborough River crossing at Fort Foster and at the battlefield site along the remains of Fort King Road. Comfortable boots or hiking shoes are recommended. We recommend that you do not wear sandals or running shoes.

d. Mosquitoes, ants, chiggers, ticks, and other insects are prevalent from March to October so insect repellent is advised. Poison ivy is also present in some of the more remote areas off the preserved site.

e. Road traffic in downtown Tampa can be heavy along normal urban schedules. Once outside of the city center further north on US 301 North, traffic lightens during the approach to Fort Foster and then to Dade Battlefield Historic State Parks.

Appendix A

Order of Battle for the Forces Involved

1. United States Army (100 enlisted, eight officers and one interpreter at time of ambush)

Major Francis Dade, Commanding

Captain Gardiner's C Company, 2d Artillery

Captain Fraser's B Company, 3d Artillery

Major Dade's Detachment B Company, 4th Infantry

Attached Soldiers from B and H Company, 2d Artillery to fill the understrength companies

Dade's Command Roll Call	
Rank and Name	**Place of Birth**
Enlisted	
Private John Barnes	Ireland
Private Donald Campbell	Scotland
Private Enoch Gates	North Carolina
Private Martin Cunningham	Pennsylvania
Private John Doughty	New York
Private Cornelius Donovan	Ireland
Private William Downs	Maryland
Private Samuel Hall	Ireland
Private Wiley Jones	North Carolina
Private John Markham	Virginia
Private Edwin Decourcey	England
Private Edward Boston	Scotland
Private Michael Kenney	Ireland
Private Anthony Laughlin	Ireland
Private John McWiggin	Ireland
Private James McDonald	Ireland
Private John McCartney	Ireland
Private Hugh Peery	Ireland
Private Patrick Rooney	Ireland
Private Richard R. Bowen	New York
Private Henry Brondan	Prussia
Private John Craig	Ireland
Private John Kerins	Ireland
Private Hugh McMee	Ireland
Private John A. Patton	Dist. Of Col.
Private Reuben Phillips	Pennsylvania

Private Thomas Thornton	Canada
Private Hiram Taylor	Pennsylvania
Private William Wright	Massachusetts
Private John Stafford	England
Private William Black	Maryland
Private Richard Burke	Ireland
Private Rufus Barton	New York
Private Owen Boyen	Ireland
Private Thomas Davis	Pennsylvania
Private Robert Green	Maryland
Private Isaac C. Grant	New York
Private Alpheus Gillert	New York
Private John Halter	Pennsylvania
Private John Hurley	Ireland
Private William Holmes	Ireland
Private Cornelius Hill	Ireland
Private Aaron Jewell	Vermont
Private Thomas Knarr	Pennsylvania
Private Robert Mulvahal	Ireland
Private William Neely	Ireland
Private Patrick Rotterty	Ireland
Private William Robertson	Scotland
Private John Riley	Scotland
Private Casper Schneder	Germany
Private William Taylor	Vermont
Private Isaac Taylor	Maryland
Private Joseph Wilson	New York
Private Orville Worcester	Vermont
Private George Bertran	Scotland
Private Ben C. Carpenter	New York
Private Patrick Cumusky	Ireland
Private Samuel E. Dodge	New York
Private William Flannagan	Ireland
Private John C. Folk	Germany
Private George Herlyhigh	Rhode Island
Private Jorden Hall	New York
Private Samuel Kinkerly	Pennsylvania
Private Jacob Kneeland	Maryland
Private Samuel Lemon	Pennsylvania
Private William Minton	New Jersey
Private Donal Monroe	New York
Private John Mulcuhy	Ireland
Private William D. Randall	New York

Private John Schaeffer	Germany
Private Henry Senram	Germany
Private Washington Tuck	Maine
Private Richard Vreeland	New Jersey
Private Samuel S. Wright	Ireland
Private John Williams	Ireland
Private Sylvester Welsh	Pennsylvania
Private Daniel Wechsong	Germany
Private George York	England
Fifer William Carney	Ireland
Drummer Charles T. Heck	Pennsylvania
Artificer George Howard	New Jersey
Artificer Henry Wagner	Pennsylvania
Noncommissioned Officers	
Sergeant Peter Thomas	Pennsylvania
Sergeant John Hood	Scotland
Sergeant Philip Cooper	Saxony
Sergeant John Louis	New Jersey
Sergeant Thomas Sarin	Ireland
Sergeant Benjamin Chapman	Rhode Island
Sergeant John Valing	Germany
Sergeant Anstin W.C. Farley	Virginia
Corporal Michael Ryan	Ireland
Corporal George G. Young	Rhode Island
Corporal Philander Wells	New York
Corporal Alexander Jones	New Jersey
Corporal Nicholas Clark	New York
Corporal James Dunlap	Maine
Officers	
Brevet Major Francis Dade	4th IN Regt.
Captain Upton S. Fraser	B Co., 3d Artillery
Captain George W. Gardiner	C Co., 2d Artillery
First Lieutenant William F. Basinger	C Co., 2d Artillery
Second Lieutenant Robert R. Mudge	B Co., 3d Artillery
Brevet Second Lieutenant R. Henderson	C Co., 2d Artillery
Brevet Second Lieutenant J.L. Keais	B Co., 3d Artillery
Assistant Surgeon John Gatlin	Medical Staff
Survivors	
Private Joseph Sprague	B Co., 3d Artillery

| Private Ransom Clark | B Co., 2d Artillery |
| Private John Thomas | B Co., 2dArtillery |

2. Seminole Forces (200-500 warriors including 50-100 mounted, and approximately 50 Africans)

Chief Micanopy, Commanding

Loosely organized Forces under Chiefs Jumper and Alligator (to include mounted element)

Appendix B

Biographical Sketches of Key Participants

Francis Langhorne Dade was born in February, 1792 in Virginia. He served in the War of 1812, always in the infantry from his first commission in the 12th Infantry Regiment but would soon find his long-lasting home under the colors of the 4th Infantry Regiment. He was serving with the 4th in Florida when he volunteered to take Captain Gardiner's command to allow the latter to have time with his ill wife. He was not a West Point educated officer.

He had extensive service in the southern garrisons and was embroiled in Florida's military adventures with the United States from the early conflicts all the way to his final battle. Dade had even served with Seminoles under his command in the vicinity of Tallahassee. He had lauded them, granting them medals for service. In 1825, Dade had undertaken a similar mission as the one he found himself on for General Clinch, to reinforce a threatened agency outpost near what would later become Fort King. At that time it had only been "Indian trails" to move on, not a developed road, but the contingent then had moved fast as they were not being slowed with a cannon.

Dade was an experienced officer. He had served extensively in Florida with Seminoles. Perhaps, though, this gave him a false sense of understanding their ways. He had also served in the War of 1812, the last "big" war of his time period that Soldiers talked about and revered. A career infantryman, he still understood the importance of a cannon on a battlefield as he demanded one accompany this march.

Perhaps too dedicated to "traditional" warfare that made careers for the professionals, Dade fell among the category of those who deeply underestimated or misjudged the Seminoles. He held a hubris that was not uncommon among the upper ranks of the US Army when it came to considering the effectiveness of "Indians" in fighting.

Regardless, Major Dade lived a life of duty to his country and never shirked from danger or risk, as clearly shown in his act of taking over for Captain Gardiner. His demand for the cannon can be judged as either a positive or a negative thing. It played a critical part in the battle, however, in reference to then-Captain Dade's previous execution of a similar mission, the absence of a cannon at that point allowed his detachment to cover the distance far faster by moving lighter and less conspicuously. Other decisions made by Dade leading up to the immediate fight itself may have been less pardonable but the students can judge for themselves.

George Washington Gardiner grew up in Kingston, New York from an affluent family. He was a lawyer's son. Gardiner was a short stocky man, said to be barely over five feet tall. He enrolled in West Point, graduating at the top of his class of 1814 in March, just in time to serve in the final months of the War of 1812.

He was an artilleryman by trade, however, Brevet Major Sylvanus Thayer, noted reformer of the Academy, recognized Gardiner's professionalism even as a young lieutenant and recommended Gardiner as temporary instructor on infantry tactics in August of 1817. In September, Gardiner found his true calling at West Point and was appointed as instructor of artillery and commandant of the cadets, known as the "God of War" by his pupils. From there, he served in various garrison posts in the northeast before temporarily leaving the military to pursue a law career as had his father.

The colors, however, would not let Captain Gardiner go and, at 42 years old, he soon found himself back in the Army doing garrison duties along both coasts of a Florida. An artilleryman all his life, Florida was not necessarily good artillery country, hence why most of the artillery was pressed into "red-legged infantryman" duties, something common in many conflicts that did not fit the "traditional" war concepts. However, as a true artillery professional, he would find a way to utilize his branch's tools as effectively as possible.

Described by Private Bemrose – Gardiner had been his first company commander when Bemrose arrived in Saint Augustine – as a "most manly and determined little character and a perfect gentleman." (Bemrose, 65). This was high praise from a young enlisted soldier of an officer in that time period.

Captain Gardiner, aside from being a proficient soldier in both infantry and artillery tactics as noted in his assignments of instruction at the Academy and his commented "gentlemanliness," was a man of strong character and devotion to both his family and to his men who he unquestioningly saw as family. As his service in the waning days of the War of 1812 and his time in garrison duties and instructing at West Point certainly prepared him, his poise, skills, and professionalism would be highest in his conduct in Dade's final battle. With his skills, specifically with use of artillery along with natural leadership attributes he demonstrated, Gardiner's role in the battle with the Seminoles would be pivotal. This was all in light of the fact that having been relieved of his requirement by Major Dade to attend to his wife but after taking care of his family, he returned to care for his other family, only speaks more of the character of Captain Gardiner.

Upton Sinclair Fraser hailed from New York City, New York and was born in 1794. Fraser was the only line officer under Major Dade's command to not be a graduate of West Point.

Though he was an artilleryman by the time of his service in Florida, Captain Fraser had begun his career as an infantry lieutenant in the Fifteenth Infantry. He joined the Fifteenth Infantry in 1814 and after only a short term with the unit, he changed branches to serve in the artillery. It was in the artillery branch that Fraser would serve through the ranks during the War of 1812. In 1828, Fraser made captain and therefore outranked Captain Gardiner by four years and was second only to Major Dade in the command on the day of the battle.

By military tradition and custom, he should have been the commander of the detachment rather than Captain Gardiner prior to Major Dade's voluntary assumption of command. In fact, Fraser had commanded Fort Brooke off and on for months leading up to the December march along Fort King Road. However, in an agreement among the officers, Fraser conceded command of the detachment to Captain Gardiner on acknowledgement of Gardiner's West Point education and training assignment and Gardiner's experience in the field.

Described by fellow officers as a brave officer and one who cared for his men, Fraser was known to have the respect of the men of his command. He was also known to be a man of letters and during the march, left hand written notes along the route for the relief column meant to follow them to Fort King. His calmness along the march was noted by those around him each night while the others showed nervousness from the situation. He remained collected and found solace in writing his messages informing the relief column of the situation and encouraging their haste. His dedication to duty and leadership by example was demonstrated up until the battle commenced, as he regularly accompanied the advance guard including on the day of the ambush.

Ransom Clark was an extraordinarily lucky individual, or as some to include himself may have concluded towards the end of his life, a cursed individual. He stood at five feet and 10 inches, a little taller than average US Soliders of the time. From New York, Clark was 23 years old when he left the gates of Fort Brooke with Dade's command. A rough character, he joined the Army for lack of other available occupation and a desire to get away from home. An artilleryman by trade, he enlisted into the 2d Artillery Regiment and served with Captain Belton but he found himself later in Captain Gardiner's C Company for the march to join General Clinch.

In Mobile Bay in early 1835, Private Clark had been on a transport ship when the boat capsized, killing all but one on board. Clark was the only survivor when he came out of the water. He considered himself a fair shot, had a steely disposition, cool-headed even if he was rough on the edges but even if he had not been rough before, a few years in a peacetime intimately small army with unrecognized frontier duty, one could become a bit rough.

Clark would leave various accounts of the battle. The first was a matter of days after the event, others years later. They virtually all were unchanged from his first report. This report of Clark was validated by the subsequent report from first person accounts of others who had first gone to the battle site, which was seemingly untouched and matched Clark's narrative, including many specifics. Clark would attempt for a time to live off the profits of his tales in print and speaking engagements as his pension from the government at eight dollars a month, though more than he was making as an enlisted soldier at five dollars a month, was not much to live off outside of military life. He would die only five years later due to complications from the wounds suffered on 28 December of which he never fully recovered.

Credit: The State Archives of Florida

Chief Micanopy, also known as the Pond-Governor, was the hereditary leader of the widely scattered and loosely organized Seminole Nation. This hereditary power came from a genealogy traced to him being a descendant of the revered Cowkeeper and of the Alachua band of the original tribes making up the Seminoles. At the time of Dade's March, he was thought by his US Government contemporaries to be about 50 years old. The issue Micanopy had was not one of hereditary leadership, he had that through blood, but was from true leadership skills. He displayed minimal traits of a great uniting leader.

He was thought personally to be lazy, more into food and drink rather than into the cares of his people. He was shorter than the average Seminole being only five feet and six inches tall compared to an average of six feet.

He was of large build, probably a trait that led to charges of laziness as he weighed a reported 250 pounds, also indicative of his indulgence in food and wine. General Clinch observed of Micanopy, "a man of but little talent or energy of character but from age and wealth, has much influence in the nation." (Mahon, 124). This influence was illustrated in that Alligator was reputed in 1837 to have said in the presence of a Washington treaty delegation that when Micanopy speaks, all listen.

Perhaps the most damning trait attributed to Micanopy, when it comes to his role as leader, was his gullibility. He was manipulated by various more junior chiefs. Though he advocated for peace, he was manipulated and at times even strong armed into violent actions against the US, both against Dade and even later at the next major engagement between the Seminoles and the US Army. Micanopy's indirect and ineffectual attempts to deter Osceola's more bombastic and robust calls for war, led to his loss of influence as an adviser or prosecutor of the war as the Seminole's grew to choose war over forced relocation. None were willing to challenge Micanopy to his face due to his hereditary and cultural prestige but his "opinions and advice were generally unheeded" Alligator later asserted. (Sprague, 93). However, Micanopy's influence and role had not faced this discredit before Dade's men encountered the Seminoles on the road to Fort King.

After Dade's Battle, Chief Micanopy would nominally lead the Seminole Nation in its revolt against the US Government's enforcement of the removal treaties until 1837 when he surrendered himself to the US Army in June and began to negotiate anew the plans to move the Seminoles westwards. He was kidnapped (or "rescued") by Osceola to further inspire resistance. He would be captured again by Brigadier General Thomas Jesup under a flag of truce, a developing US military method to capture key Seminole leaders even though this was sharply against the accepted ethics of war. Though he had already agreed to peace once before being taken by Osceola, Micanopy was, in December 1838, sent to prison at Fort Moultrie, South Carolina where he remained until he and nearly 200 other prisoners were shipped to the new Indian Territory the Seminoles were to share with their longtime nemesis and parent tribe, the Creek. He died on the 2nd of January in 1849 at Fort Gibson, Oklahoma.

Micanopy's principle subordinates at the battle were two junior chiefs, Jumper and Alligator. Osceola was usually the main manipulator of Micanopy, bending his ear (or arm in some cases) to his point of view. However, Osceola was undertaking the other half of the Seminole plan. Osceola would not be present at the battle with Dade as he was focusing on the other task, that of targeting the political power of the US Government in Florida, the Indian Affairs agent Wiley Thompson.

Credit: The State Archives of Florida

Jumper, or Ote Emathla (on the left in this image) was said to be cunning, intelligent and outspoken – a manipulator of Micanopy – as well as self-absorbed and eloquent. He was said to be about 40 years old at the time of the battle with Dade. He was known to be individually a brave warrior. His battlefield leadership and outspoken persuasiveness were to be critical to the Seminole actions.

Jumper continued to wage war against the US Army after Dade's Battle and was later captured and shipped west to the new lands promised to the Seminoles. Once there, Jumper solidified his leadership and would become head chief of the Seminoles upon the death of his brother in 1849. The following year, Chief Jumper led a delegation back to Florida to try to convince the few remaining Seminoles to leave the territory and join the rest of the Seminole Nation out west and avert another Seminole war. However, there was still a Third Seminole War.

When the American Civil War broke out in 1861, he organized an alliance with the Confederate States of America when the Seminole Nation was split with varying allegiances. He served as a major with the First

Battalion of Mounted Seminole Rifles and later obtained a colonelcy in the First Regiment of Seminole Volunteers and served in numerous skirmishes in the western theater of war. He died at his home on the 21st of September in 1896.

Alligator, or **Halpatter Tustenuggee** was one of the planners of the Seminole operation. He was known to be shrewd and calculating. Like Micanopy, he was short for a Seminole standing at barely five feet. Perhaps this led to his over compensation as he was said to be a self-styled comedian in all the meetings with the white delegations. He was said to also display delusions of grandeur, grand-standing in dealings with whites specifically. Some of this bombast could be attributed to his ability to speak English and his amiable nature as recorded by some of the delegates. Even they, though, were said to recognize his manipulative qualities and his fellow Seminoles were said to be wary of his cunning and political skills. He was estimated to be about 40 years of age at the time of the outbreak of hostilities.

Credit: The Smithsonian

The role Alligator played in the battle with Dade's troopers was a strong tactical influence as evidenced by the Seminole's actions. Alligator was said to hold extensive knowledge of the countryside and in tactics, demonstrated by his regular use of flanking maneuvers, coordinated assaults and retreats and even feints. He was known as "a dangerous foe" by contemporary US Army officers. (Sprague, 97-98). These skills were displayed first at Dade's final battle and again throughout the war until Alligator fought his final battle. Similar to Private Clark, however, it was not just Alligator's actions on the field of battle that made him important to Dade's Battle; it was also his being the only Seminole account of the battle left to posterity. Whether or not this was due to his ability to speak English, the fact of Alligator's account of the fight makes his role and place in the battle of important interest.

Alligator more than either of the other chiefs at Dade's Battle, would go on to serve extensively in the Second Seminole War. He was present at every major battle from the Battle of the Withlacoochie only days after Dade's Battle to the Battle of Camp Izard's and the only large set-piece battle of the war, the Battle of Okeechobee on Christmas day in 1837. Shortly after the Battle of Okeechobee, of which he played a major role, he surrendered, tired of the killing, and willingly went west. He was brought back to Florida as part of a Seminole commission in late 1841 to convince the remaining Seminole holdouts to move west. He was said to have been successful and himself would return to the territory in Oklahoma. There he continued to advocate for the recognition of a Seminole Nation separate from the Creek Nation in the Oklahoma (Indian) Territory. History would last hear of him in 1857 when he sent his children to missionary school but his actual date of death is unknown.

Appendix C
Historical Maps

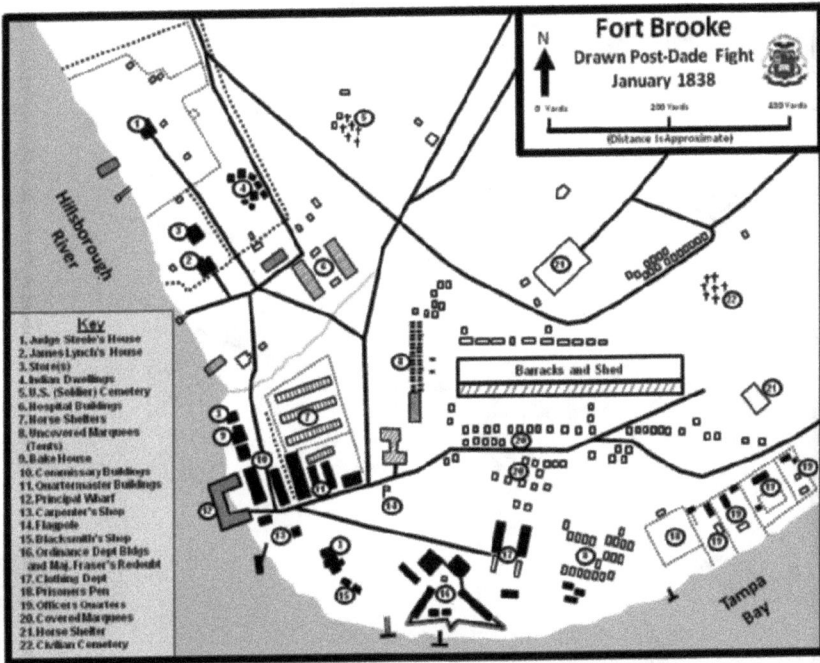

Fort Brooke
Drawn Post-Dade Fight
January 1838

0 Yards   200 Yards   450 Yards
(Distance Is Approximate)

Hillsborough River

Tampa Bay

Barracks and Shed

Key
1. Judge Steele's House
2. James Lynch's House
3. Store(s)
4. Indian Dwellings
5. U.S. (Soldier) Cemetery
6. Hospital Buildings
7. Horse Shelters
8. Uncovered Marquees (Tents)
9. Bake House
10. Commissary Buildings
11. Quartermaster Buildings
12. Principal Wharf
13. Carpenter's Shop
14. Flagpole
15. Blacksmith's Shop
16. Ordnance Dept Bldgs and Maj. Fraser's Redoubt
17. Clothing Dept
18. Prisoners Pen
19. Officers Quarters
20. Covered Marquees
21. Horse Shelter
22. Civilian Cemetery

Map 1. Fort Brooke.

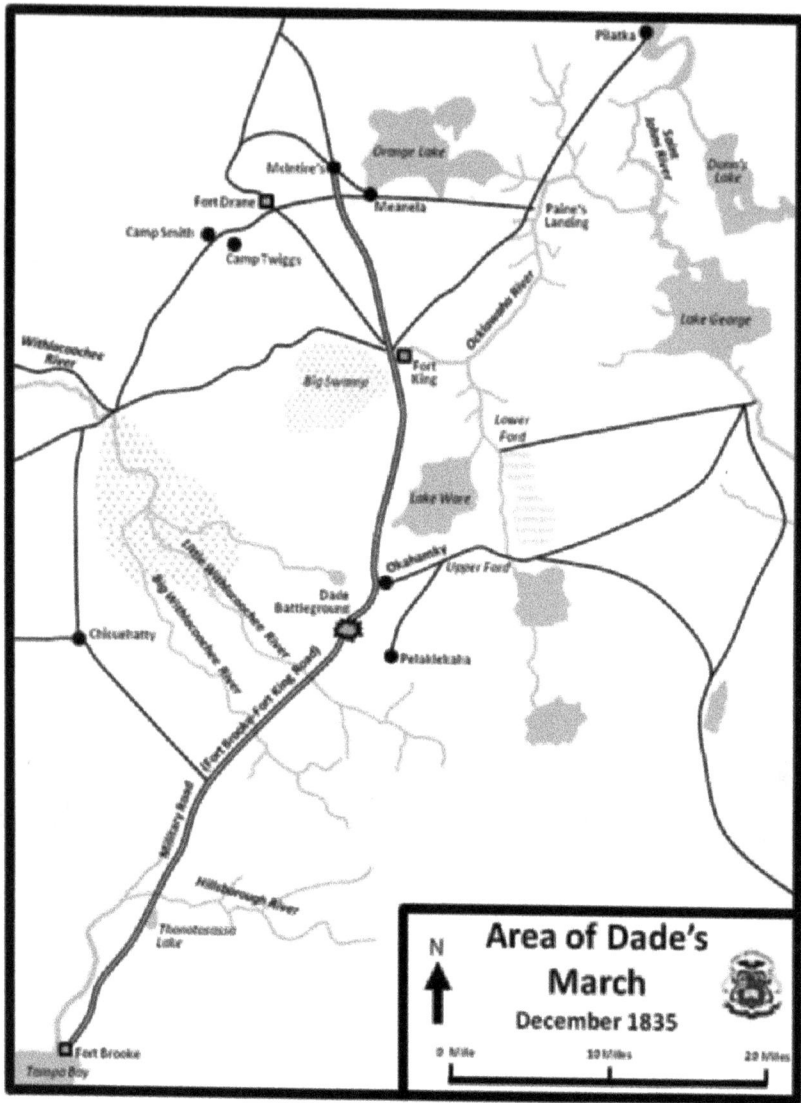

Map 2. Area of Dade's March.

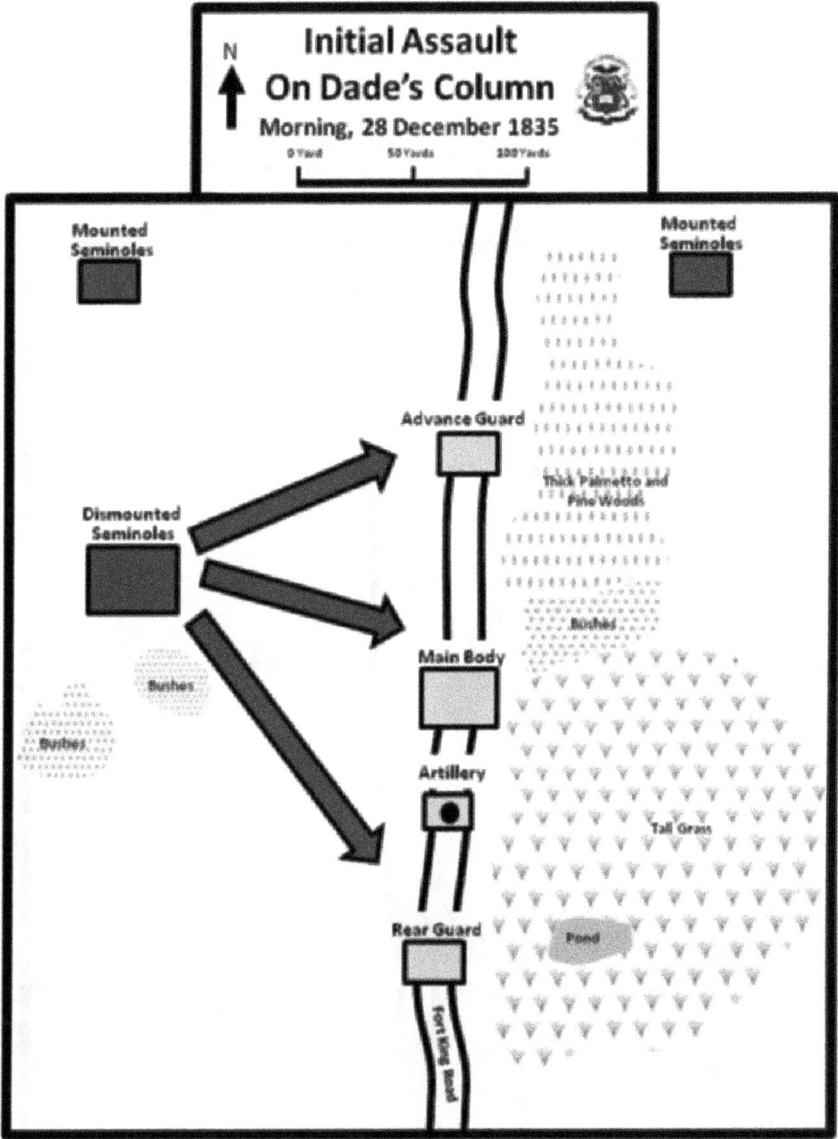

Map 3. Initial Assault.

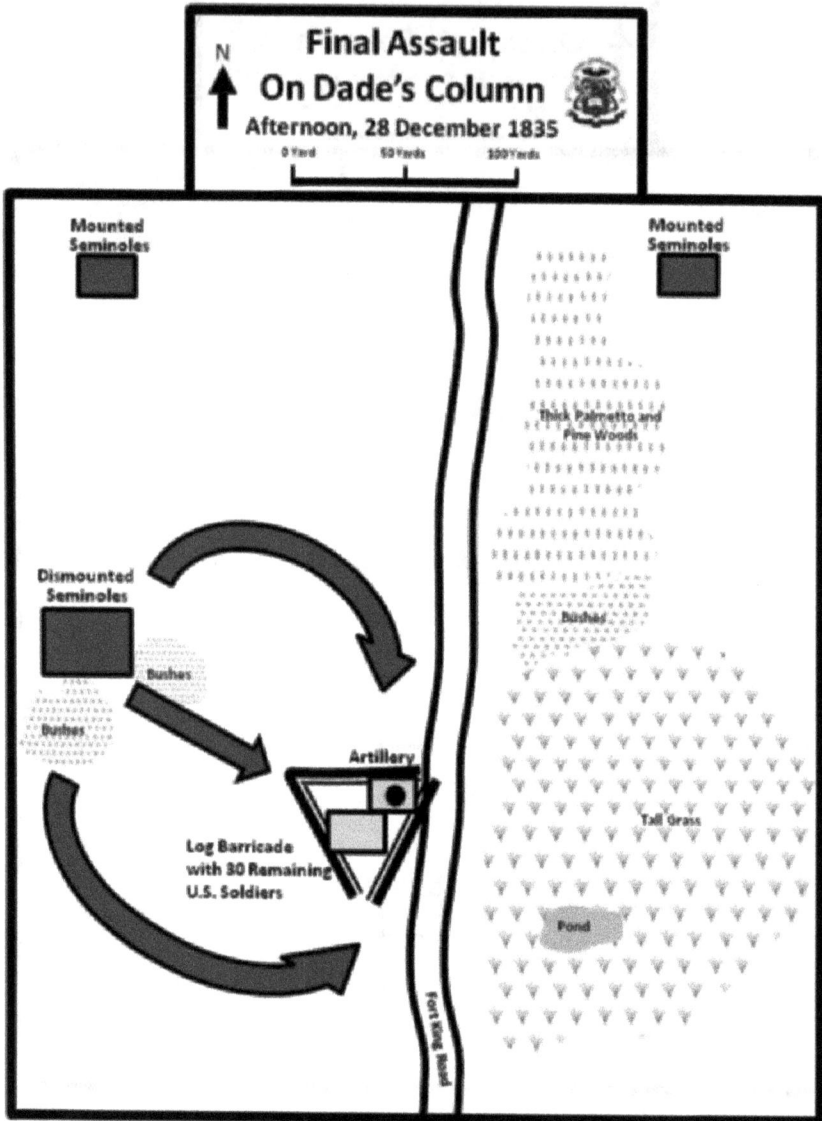

Map 4. The Final Assault.

Bibliography

Primary Accounts of the Second Seminole War. Only works used in the writing of this handbook are listed.

Bemrose, John. *Reminiscences of the Second Seminole War*. Edited with an Introduction and Postscript by John K. Mahon. Tampa, FL: University of Tampa Press. 2001.

Cohen, M.M. *Notices of Florida and the Campaigns*. Charleston, SC: Burges and Honour. 1836.

McCall, George A. *Letters from the Frontiers*. Philadelphia, PA: J.B. Lippincott and Company. 1868.

Potter, Woodburne. *The War in Florida*. Baltimore, MD: Lewis and Coleman. 1836.

Sprague, John T. *Origin, Progress and Conclusion of the Florida War*. D. Broadway, NY: Appleton and Company. 1847.

Stoddard, Amos. *Exercise for Garrison and Field Ordnance Together with Maneuvers*. New York, NY: Pelsue & Gold. 1812.

Secondary Sources of the Second Seminole War. As with the primary accounts, this list consists of only works used in the writing of this handbook.

Covington, James W. *The Seminoles of Florida*. Gainesville, FL: University Press of Florida. 1993.

Cubberly, Frederick. *The Dade Massacre*. Washington: Government Printing Office. 1921.

Graves, Donald E. "Field Artillery of the War of 1812: Equipment, Organization, Tactics and Effectiveness": in *Arms Collecting*, Vol. 30, No. 2 (May 1992), p. 39-48.

Hall, John. "Dubious Means and Unworthy Ends: Colonel William Worth's Campaign to End the Second Seminole War": in *War Termination: The Proceedings of the War Termination Conference, USMA*. Edited by Mathew Moten. Fort Leavenworth, KS: Combat Studies Institute Press. 2010.

Hsieh, Wayne Wei-siang. *West Pointers and the Civil War: The Old Army in War and Peace*.

Chapel Hill, NC: The University North Carolina Press. 2009.

Laumer, Frank. *Dade's Last Command*. Gainesville, FL: University Press of Florida. 1995.

Mahon, John K. *History of the Second Seminole War, 1835-1842* (revised edition). Gainesville, FL: University of Florida Press. 1967.

McReynolds, Edwin C. *The Seminoles*. Norman, OK: University of Oklahoma Press. 1957.

Missall, John and Mary Lou Missal. *The Seminole Wars: America's Longest Indian Conflict*. Gainesville, FL: University Press of Florida, 2004.

Webb, George. "Dade Battlefield Staff Ride Questions." Message to Michael Anderson. 19 December 2012. E-mail.